ALL

—

THE

—

HARD

—

THINGS

SARAH FREYMUTH

HARVEST HOUSE PUBLISHERS
EUGENE, OREGON

For bulk, special sales, or ministry purchases, please call 1-800-547-8979.
Email: CustomerService@hhpbooks.com

Cover design by Faceout Studio, Tim Green

Cover images © ArtMari, tets / Shutterstock

Interior design by Chad Dougherty

All the Hard Things
Copyright © 2026 by Sarah Freymuth
Published by Harvest House Publishers
Eugene, Oregon 97408
www.harvesthousepublishers.com

ISBN 978-0-7369-9199-5 (Hardcover)
ISBN 978-07369-9200-8 (eBook)

Library of Congress Control Number: 2025937066

Printed in China

25 26 27 28 29 30 31 32 33 34 / RDS / 10 9 8 7 6 5 4 3 2 1

For my grandpa, Don Rennicke—
the first true champion of my writing.

And for those who walk the valley—
may you stay close to the Shepherd.

CONTENTS

DOWN THE RAPIDS: SITUATIONAL STRUGGLES

BROKEN BRANCHES: RELATIONAL STRAIN

UP THE MOUNTAIN: GOOD HARD THINGS

THROUGH THE NIGHT, INTO MORNING: GREAT IS HIS FAITHFULNESS

INTRODUCTION

A Pilgrimage Begins

PRAISE THE LORD; PRAISE GOD OUR SAVIOR! FOR EACH
DAY HE CARRIES US IN HIS ARMS. **PSALM 68:19** NLT

The sun swings below the horizon, slowly extinguishing the day. Shadows stretch, like extended fingers of the branches of beech, juniper, and oak trees, all knotted together in the woods that have lined your pathway for longer than you'd like to admit.

Dusk will soon settle in, hiding the wildflowers and tall grass, though the sweet scent of them still lingers.

Where am I? You try to remember the way you've walked today, look for any signposts that signal a location. But you have no map, and you don't know the destination. You set out on this pilgrimage to make sense of all the hard things that have worn you bone-weary. Every step is new ground covered; there are no instructions for times like these.

Water from your canteen runs cold and smooth down your throat, relieving the physical thirst, yet your spiritual appetite still pants. "Where are you, God?" you whisper to the smattering of stars manifesting across the darkening sky. You long for his voice, a reassurance that he sees you even though you have lost your way. But the rustle of leaves and high buzz of crickets are the only response.

You never asked for this road, never wanted to go through this life with the weight of disappointment, pain, and loss heavy on your heart. It's exhausting, and through the trees and meadow, a thin fog is rolling in.

"God, please," you murmur, before settling into a plush spot in the grass. "Help me through."

Eyelids lower, heart still asking what words cannot say. Sleep comes, with weary hope for a new day tomorrow.

What do you do when you get the news you never expected to hear? Or the news you've always dreaded to receive? When you've clung to a wild hope that seems to grow smaller with each new month or passing year?

Confidence wavers, and we can even experience a crisis of faith. *Where is God in all this?* we ask. *Is he really invested that much in my life that he would leave me in this suffering? He has the power to put an end to it, so what's the hold up?*

"In this world, you will have trouble," Jesus says to us (John 16:33). But in the next breath, he tells us to rest easy, for he has overcome the trouble-twisted world.

Does it feel like it? When we stare into a cavern of grief from the loss of a beloved one, or a medical diagnosis with a wicked track history, we're faced with a faith that either holds up or unfolds, collapses or expands. It can get muddy when the platitudes we've held don't seem to holdup under the sheer force of what's threatening to knock us down.

Do we have breath to murmur our doubt, our grief, our fears? Can we muster up any movement at all to make our way to the top of this long stretching summit? Peaks and valleys, shadows and storms, the surges and quakes of the earth beneath our feet. Will we ever stand on solid ground again?

The hard things feel unbearable. But they will not overtake us. The God of this universe always has his grip on us.

Do not fear, for I am with you;
do not be dismayed, for I am your God.
I will strengthen you and help you; I will uphold you
with my righteous right hand.

ISAIAH 41:10

Welcome to *All the Hard Things: 50 Days Through the Valley*. Together, we are going to walk through the circumstances of life that are sharp and split us open, and we are going to search for God's presence with us in these lowlands. I'm not claiming any answers or expertise. I'm not going to stand on stage and give you a pep talk filled with self-help mantras and frame up the benefits of positive thinking. But I *am* going to hold your hand and walk with you as a fellow sojourner seeking the heart of God in all the hard.

I've been in the deep shadows and valleys more times over the last decade than I'd like, and the more I make my way into the thicket of life, the more twisting and overgrown brush I encounter. Sometimes I lose the trail altogether.

Sometimes, there are no good answers. And, I hate to say, sometimes there are no answers at all.

The unanswered leaves us in quite a vulnerable position. But, if I'm to offer any hope, it is that there is a vulnerable God who, unfathomably, enters into our pain and presses his heart right up to ours. I know at times it feels like he is a thousand miles away, watching with only mild interest in reaching out to help. But the thing about faith is, we get to a point where we can't go off our feelings anymore. We have to stand on the things we've been taught, look back on what we've experienced.

Faith is a remembrance of God's faithfulness in the past, not only in the lives of our spiritual forefathers and mothers in the Bible, but in our own lives as well. And it's an anchoring to his Word, a clinging to his character where we count on him to show up as who he says he is. We hold him to it, by faith. And we look forward when we cannot see an end to the hurt, where clouds have not yet parted and the weariness lingers, believing that just because we do not yet see doesn't mean more will not be revealed.

God is after our hearts, as well as the strengthening and growth of our character. He made us his image bearers, and for us humans, character growth is often a process of restoration rather than an immediate change. And his means to get us there, for some upside-down reason, is to take us through the unthinkable, the heartbreak and loss, disappointment, and pain in all different ways.

This is a pilgrimage through all the hard things. But we are going to navigate our way through. It won't be easy, and there is no direct path, but we're going to keep walking by leaning on the promises of God, remembering how he has gotten his children through hard things before, and he certainly won't stop with your story. We may be hurting, but we will not be left behind.

Our hearts are set on pilgrimage. Let's begin.

IN ROLLS THE FOG:

SPIRITUAL DISCONTENT

———

Slender fingers of fog weave around the waves of air and through the woods. Moments before, we could see an expanse of tall grass, puffed clouds, and a cluster of soft evergreen trees, but now they are encased in gray shadows. The fog blocks our way, makes the ground beneath us tender. I'm uncertain where to place my feet, and my arms involuntarily stretch in front of me so I don't run into something solid. Your eyesight isn't any better, and I know you're looking for an explanation for the sudden appearance of this encompassing fog.

All this gray—it's numbing. Are we losing our bearings? Can we remember the way we were told to go, though we can no longer see the road? This new confusion startles and disorients, and we claw our way forward with trepidation.

God's voice is hidden in the thick silence of this fog. We plead for him to take us out of this mist and into visibility, to hold our hand so we can have sunshine warm our faces.

We're made for relationship with the Triune God who expresses himself through relationship and communion. Our hearts are inclined to hook to his, and when we are unable to discern his nearness, it's enough to send us spinning, lost and lonely.

It's here, in the fog of spiritual discontent, where we examine what we honestly believe. When we enter into those seasonal spaces of the dark night of the soul and God seems distant and mysterious, we wonder if something has happened to us that makes our faith falter. When the floor drops beneath us and we stumble around, sometimes we have to shed our old ways of finding God and hold to a new way of believing.

1

HIS LIGHT, A BEACON

Reorienting After Losing Our Way

WE SEE LIGHT. **PSALM 36:9**

I struggle with the weight of wandering, fight with a tightness in my chest, a veil over my heart. This dim light of a season full of fatigue, head fog, and anxiety stretches on longer than I ever would have imagined. This is not something of my choosing, but God knows this. He knows the inside of my heart, the private corners I don't even like to share with myself. He sees my scared suspicions of his absence, fears that force their way into my head, the patterns of thinking I can't seem to stop. I thought he would give me a better light to see through my suffering, not to dampen my faith and dizzy me with a silence only broken by my exasperated cries for clarity.

Losing direction when our spiritual senses seem to go out is unnerving and disorienting.

But there *is* hope; God has guaranteed it (Proverbs 23:18). I am an active participant in this stretching, this suffering. These growing pains result in my good, even in the middle of this process. Even when there's no time frame that shows the end. Even when faith must overcome feeling, or a lack thereof. The fog over both mind and soul will not last forever. Though it is hard to discern his presence or navigate this unknown, he is providing for me right here, right now. Holding on to me when I have no strength to which I can cling on my own.

I lift my heart, my mind, to the sky that is a tranquil blue today. It's been so gray for so long, low-hanging clouds dampening the view. But light lies behind the clouds.

We can see a step beyond where we are when we look for his light, the glow that brings illumination in the darkness. He has led us into this darkness, the bleak caverns that cover our sight, but he has also given us himself, a guiding light that leads us into the life he has in store, one that results in our good and his glory. Dimly lit as it may be, we still can *see* hope before we feel it.

Every day, we have a choice: curl up and feebly live through the day, or fight for the faith we know is there despite what we cannot see. Faith becomes sight, and the sliver of light he gives today will grow brighter tomorrow. It's the mindset of more: more trust, more faith, more of him making a way.

The angel of the Lord encamps around those who
fear him, and he delivers them.

PSALM 34:7

With the God of the universe beside us, what can we truly fear?

Today let's choose to hold to the light, to fasten our eyes on a blue sky, even if the window might say otherwise. God is faithful. The darkness does not last. We can open to that tightness in our chest, acknowledge our fear, our disappointment, our sense that this is a new path of faith we've never walked. We can give grace to ourselves that we might not have allowed in a long time. Grace grows to acceptance, and we release the burdens we were never meant to bear.

We can shift our hearts to believe beyond the unbearable. Believe his presence is the fountain of sustaining waters springing forth in our souls (John 7:38). Believe he is making a way, even in the midst of what feels broken. Believe his light is strong enough to penetrate the blackest night.

With you is the fountain of life;
in your light we see light.

PSALM 36:9

His is the light that sees us through, even when all looks shadowed—*especially* then. When I don't understand, I choose to obey anyway. At just the right time, his light will break through, and goodness will once again flood my soul. Joy will come in the morning (Psalm 30:5). Sorrow will give way to singing. In my weakness, his strength becomes my lifeline. He brings his light right on time. I take hold of this comfort and let my chest expand a little more, allowing release.

REFLECT

What verse can you hold to when you need your faith to be bigger than your lack of feeling?

How can you begin to tune your eyes to see the light of God around you?

LINGER

Psalm 36:7-9; Psalm 40:1-2; Galatians 3:6

RESPOND

Lord, I feel so weak and uncertain right now. I am forging through the fog in me, and I fear I have lost my way to you. In your light I see light; illuminate my heart to take hope that this heaviness will not last, and you will yet again revive my heart and faith. In Jesus' name, amen.

PRAISE

"Dear Heartache" by 7 Hills Worship and Rachel Morley

2

RECOVERING FROM LIFE

Seeking Rest When We're Weary

I WILL GIVE YOU REST. **MATTHEW 11:28**

Life comes too fast. Too full. Culture keeps moving forward at the speed of light, but I am blinded in my search for God's presence. I can't quite seem to find his voice amid the sounds in my head and distractions on the screen. *Where are you, Lord? I can't hear you in all the noise.* I long for more of him, but today he feels like more shadow than shape, and the search leaves me exhausted.

I am tired of trying to say the right prayers, read the right Scripture, and adjust my heart to where I think it needs to be to receive words from God again. It's all too much. I am spiritually starved, stuck in my striving, weary from doing good and wondering what more I need to find true rest.

Are you tired? Worn out? Burned out on religion?
Come to me. Get away with me and you'll recover your
life. I'll show you how to take a real rest. Walk with
me and work with me—watch how I do it. Learn the
unforced rhythms of grace. I won't lay anything heavy or

ill-fitting on you. Keep company with me and you'll
learn to live freely and lightly.

MATTHEW 11:28-30 MSG

Tired? Burned out? Done with doing? We've let society tell us the steps we need to take in order to find grace and closeness with the Lord. We have blocked out the gentle voice that reaches into our weary hearts with a breath of fresh perspective.

Come to the Lord, all who are weary. All who are worn out from wondering whether God truly sees this situation and why he's taking his time responding. God gives great rest, if only we would still our souls long enough to let him whisper.

Spiritual renewal awakens a spark in us that has long laid too dormant. Defenses down, heart open, we move to a posture of receiving what God wants to share with us.

My heart is not proud, LORD, my eyes are not haughty;
I do not concern myself with great matters or things too
wonderful for me. But I have calmed and quieted myself,
I am like a weaned child with its mother;
like a weaned child I am content.

PSALM 131:1-2

No more striving. No more plowing through our quiet time as one more thing to get done. The Lord offers us a way to real rest, as we hitch our hearts to his and walk in his ways, match his cadence, tune our ears to his voice. He wants to *ease* our burdens, not add to them. To slow our minds that are always in motion, let's lean in close to the one who offers us a true and proper way of living. There's great freedom when we stop *working* for God and start *walking* with him.

Clear out the clutter that's been corroding your heart and mind. One worry, one task on the to-do list at a time, release it to the Father. Set it aside and make room for silence. Don't be afraid to sit in it, even if it feels a bit uncomfortable. God is near. Immanuel is with you. Maybe to begin, all you need is to sit in quiet and let your body untangle from the stress of constant strain. God holds you while you allow yourself to *be*, and that is the best place to find yourself.

He says, "Be still, and know that I am God;
I will be exalted among the nations,
I will be exalted in the earth."

PSALM 46:10

Be still. There's so much God longs to show us when we take the time to slow down from the pace of our lives and our to-do lists, sit with him, and notice what he wants to share. Subtly, when we let ourselves sit in quiet, we begin to see the Lord's shape from the shadows. We realize he's been here the entire time, but now we have the spiritual space and eyes to see.

REFLECT

How has your life gotten too busy? Can you see where you have been striving for God rather than sitting with him?

Take five minutes in silence. How does your body feel?
Where can you sense God's presence?

LINGER

Exodus 14:14; Proverbs 3:24; Luke 10:38-39

RESPOND

*Father, all this striving is stretching me thin. I keep doing more
and more, and the level of noise I'm in constantly chips away at
my soul. I am not meant to keep up with all this activity, and I
miss you. Hold me close and help me sit with you and share my
heart. I want your unforced rhythms of grace. In Jesus' name,
amen.*

PRAISE

"Closer" by Lifepoint Worship

3

MAKE A WAY IN ME

Looking to God for Comfort

BE STILL. **MARK 4:39**

Another night too quiet for comfort. Another night left alone with my thoughts, my failings, my doubts. This stretch of spiritual unknown is unnerving. It's gone on a bit too long for my liking, and I am unsettled by God's silence in my struggle. Why won't this pain end? Why can't I know the time stamp for a solution? Why must I make my way through this maze of unknowing that stretches through the months? My soul shakes, unsteady. I long for reprieve from this pain, from the heaviness stretched across my chest and the hours spent tossing in bed, longing for peace that just isn't coming.

Have you faced a time of spiritual discomfort, an unease in your heart that doesn't seem to settle? We wonder why God is taking his time, why he doesn't answer us when we call out. We can tell ourselves about his promises in the Bible that say he is always with us, but in the blackness of early morning hours when nothing can soothe our scratched hearts, what we know wrestles with what we believe.

You, Lord, hear the desire of the afflicted; you encourage them, and you listen to their cry.

PSALM 10:17

The tears stream, the heart twists, and we grow weary. But God is faithful, even in the midst of the raging storm. He turns his ear to hear the afflicted, the ones he loves who are bent low with worry and discouragement. Not one tear cried has gone unnoticed (Psalm 56:8), not one tear of the heart has gone untouched. The Lord loves you too much to leave you in your misery. He is the God who calms the seas; surely, he can calm the sea in me. He can calm the storm in you. He is the one who literally calms the storm:

> That day when evening came, he said to his disciples, "Let us go over to the other side." Leaving the crowd behind, they took him along, just as he was, in the boat. There were also other boats with him. A furious squall came up, and the waves broke over the boat, so that it was nearly swamped. Jesus was in the stern, sleeping on a cushion. The disciples woke him and said to him, "Teacher, don't you care if we drown?"
>
> He got up, rebuked the wind and said to the waves, "Quiet! Be still!" Then the wind died down and it was completely calm.
>
> He said to his disciples, "Why are you so afraid? Do you still have no faith?"
>
> They were terrified and asked each other, "Who is this? Even the wind and the waves obey him!" (Mark 4:35-41).

Who is this? This is the one who climbs into our boat of belief and combats the winds of doubt wreaking havoc in us. He can say to our mind and soul, "Quiet! Be still" (Mark 4:39). He can help us be still and know his goodness, his timing, his ways, and presence. Amid the hard, we can ask for joy and hope, a sound mind (2 Timothy 1:7), and a secure heart.

Our good Father's plans for our lives are good, for hope and a future (Jeremiah 29:11). He is making a way, helping us get through this storm, and soothing us as he guides us through the waves. He calms us through the middle of the water, when there is no shore in sight, when we are most fearful and frantic for land. He knows the waters well. He knows *us* well. He calls out our name and speaks to the deep places where he knows what we need better than we do. He is our counselor and comfort, our fixed point on a shaky axis.

He is the God who makes a way and surrounds us. He is the one who will calm this sea within and carry us to steady ground. He is our rock and firm foundation (Psalm 61:2) and gives us a glimmer of hope on the horizon. This night will not last forever. Though waves dash against the boat, the rocks, our minds and hearts, he will take us safely through.

May this be my prayer and yours: *You are the God who calms the seas; surround me with your strength, my God and Deliverer. Clear the path, the storm, and make a way in me.*

REFLECT

What are the storms in your life right now? How can you bring God into them?

The Lord is able to calm the sea in you—let him in the boat and trust he who is making a way. Take some time to meditate on this truth and consider what it means for the storms you're facing today.

LINGER

Psalm 107:29-30; Matthew 7:24-27; Luke 8:22-25

RESPOND

Lord, the waves of hurt, unrest, and confusion crash over me. I am over my head and fearful where these waters will take me. Climb in my boat, Lord, and soothe me with your presence. You calm the seas of this earth; please, calm this sea in me. Make a way for your grace, your love, and your hope. Make a way in me. In Jesus' name, amen.

PRAISE

"Peace Be Still" by Hope Darst

4

WINTERS OF THE HEART

Armoring Up to Strengthen Our Faith

HE HELPS ME. **PSALM 28:7**

We're finally seeing hints of spring after a long Wisconsin winter: branches with the tiniest of buds, warmer winds that aren't laced with ice as they whip across my face, and slowly but surely, a sun that's staying up in the sky later and later into the evening hours.

But how we fought the dark, dreary drudgery of months that buried us inside as we huddled under blankets and layers, weary with longing for the days when we could fill our lungs with fresh air again. I'm worn out, especially after being depleted by anxiety and depression while rebuilding from the aftermath of a year of health scares for my husband and myself.

This world can make me feel weak. How about you? From the constant demands of family life and taking care of others, to the cyclical toll of hearing about tragedy after tragedy in the news—it's too much for our weary hearts to hold. If you're like me, sometimes you're not sure you can take one step more. Your faith can feel so frail when you're pouring out all your energy simply to make it through the day.

The enemy does his best to keep us down, with discouragement and distraction coming at us from all angles. As this steady stream of trials washes over our hearts, we're left exposed and worn down, in desperate need of reprieve.

But God knew we'd face adversity, that inevitable winter of our hearts. So, he's given us tactics and tools to remember who he is and to call on him to come into the battle.

Psalm 7:10 reminds us God is our shield, among many other things: "My shield is God Most High, who saves the upright in heart."

Impenetrable. Strong. Resilient. God never grows weary, and he never gets tired of coming to our rescue. In fact, he delights in it.

God fights for us as we rely on him (Deuteronomy 3:22). So while he fights our battles and breaks down our hardships, our greatest weapon against adversity is our shield of faith in him (Ephesians 6:16).

The function of a shield is to keep the enemy from getting to us. It stands between us and our adversary. Because the Lord is our shield (Psalm 28:7), he protects us from lies and attacks of the enemy. With the Lord at work for us, nothing can cut us so deeply that he cannot heal those wounds as his truth and banner hold steady above us. He is our steady hand and ever-present help in times of trouble (Psalm 46:1). He gives us the grace to endure the battle and offers the hope of a lasting victory.

The Lord is my strength and my shield; my heart trusts
in him, and he helps me. My heart leaps for joy,
and with my song I praise him.

PSALM 28:7

But we have a role in this too—we battle alongside God in a combined partnership. He does the great work of fighting for us and offering protection, and we have the task of lifting that shield of faith over our minds, our hearts, and our bodies. We hold to his Word, reminding ourselves who God is: Strong Tower (Proverbs 18:10), Refuge (Psalm 9:9), Redeemer (Isaiah 41:14), Shepherd (John 10:11), Deliverer (Psalm 18:2), Defender (Psalm 18:2), among many other characteristics. And we repeat truth to ourselves over and over throughout the day, even through the night (Psalm 130:6).

God has equipped us with every piece of armor (Ephesians 6:11-18) and truth we need to find victory when the thunder cloud of negative self-talk rolls in, and when the unexpected sucker punch of bad news threatens to drag us down. The more we exercise our faith, the more we begin to build our strength and stand firm against the enemy's schemes and the world's chaos.

*You, L*ORD*, are a shield around me, my glory,*
the One who lifts my head high.

PSALM 3:3

Weary one, pull out your shield. Lift it in front of your mind and heart. Keep it raised forever high.

REFLECT

What battle(s) are you currently facing in your own life? How does knowing God is for you change the way you approach this battle?

What truth of God's can you speak over your heart and mind today? Which pieces of the armor of God do you most want to wield in this season? Make a list of God's attributes and repeat them to yourself whenever you find yourself getting tired or afraid. This will help you hold high your shield of faith.

LINGER

Psalm 138:7; Isaiah 54:17; Romans 8:31

RESPOND

Father, I feel so weak. My heart feels battered, and while spring is coming, renewal still feels so far away for me. I'm tired. My faith is tender. Would you help me lift up and keep raised my shield of faith? Would you be my shield of protection, my defender, the one who fights my battle? Thank you that you are strong and steadfast and that you love protecting Your children. In Jesus' name, amen.

PRAISE

"Head to Toe (The Armor of God Song)" by Christy Nockels

5

TO THE DEPTHS

Bringing Our Anxieties to God

YOU ARE THERE. **PSALM 139:8**

April 2022

I wake to rain coursing down from a slate gray sky, pooling in the streets, strengthening the already green grass and grove of trees in the mini park in front of city hall I see from my window. After drinking coffee and making scones that turn out more like lemon blueberry pancakes, I settle into my office to finish my taxes and start my work.

In this heavy season, within this ordinary day's load, a nagging feeling pushes on my chest. How can I keep climbing up this steep incline of life, toggling between swirling concerns about health and income and chores and errands, my mind endlessly trying to stay afloat in a sea of schedules and to-do lists? It's a lot. It pushes me further and further to the depths.

This is all of us, though, isn't it? Wondering and worrying, uncertain about the combined strain of outside forces and inner storms. We worry about finances, how bills will be paid, how we will ever get ahead, whatever "ahead" means to us. What do we do when there's so much in the world that threatens to take us under? And where is God in it all?

We sag beneath this steady stream of suffering and sorrow, left afraid that there will be no lightening of the loads we've found ourselves under. Where do we turn for relief, for deliverance? To the God who has plumbed the depths and searched the skies to show us grace.

Where can I go from your Spirit?
Where can I flee from your presence?
If I go up to the heavens, you are there; if I make my bed
in the depths, you are there. If I rise on the wings of the
dawn, if I settle on the far side of the sea, even there your
hand will guide me, your right hand will hold me fast.

PSALM 139:7-10

If we go into the loneliest crevice of the ocean, he remains. If we soar to the heights of the morning rays, there he is. He is ever mindful and attentive, holding us, watching us, protecting us. The God who breathed this universe into being also brought you into it with care and craftsmanship. He took great effort to form you (Jeremiah 1:5) exactly as you are.

Everyday hardships and struggles, even when they may seem insignificant, still catch the ear of God. From the moment we wake to the time we climb into bed, God sees us through the hourly decisions, thoughts, piles of to-do's, and tiny inconveniences. When we are overwhelmed, God longs for us to let him in on our struggles. When we are navigating a season where even the simplest tasks leave us feeling strained, God wants us to tell him when we don't have the capacity to carry on alone, to confide in him when we feel exhausted and anxious. Our struggles don't need to be earth-shattering for us to share them with God; remember, his goal for us is intimacy and transformation, and that comes when we can be honest about what weighs us down.

We are deeply known. Every cell, every smile, every semblance of fear settling in our hearts. God is the God who knows us, who loves us and longs for us to embrace that love. He desires intimacy with us so ardently that he sent his Son to walk among us and take the penalty for our sins on a cross (John 3:16-17). Our shame—erased. Our guilt—gone. We are welcomed into his family forever.

You have searched me, Lord, and you know me.
You know when I sit and when I rise; you perceive my
thoughts from afar. You discern my going out and my
lying down; you are familiar with all my ways.
Before a word is on my tongue you, Lord, know it
completely. You hem me in behind and before,
and you lay your hand upon me.

PSALM 139:1-5

We are never abandoned by God, no matter what our circumstances may suggest. He has made sure that nothing can or will ever separate us from his love (Romans 8:38-39). We may feel like we keep falling, but in Christ, we are more than conquerors (Romans 8:37). Nothing can separate us (Romans 8:39) from the love of the God who knows and sees us. There is no distance too great nor trial too terrible to take us from the unwavering love of our good Father. We are sealed and guarded in the grace of God through Jesus, and we can hold this light of truth out in front of us when we've stumbled into the darkness.

God is with us, in ways seen and unseen, in moments of confusion and elation, in the assurance of his presence through his Word, willing to go to the heights or to the depths with us. Remember that

God is with you. When you fall to the depths, settle in. God has you and will raise you back up once again.

REFLECT

Do you feel like you are in a place where God cannot reach you? What do the truths of Psalm 139 say instead?

Let the Lord remind you that you are always on his mind and wherever you go, he is already there. Take some time to memorize one verse from Scripture that helps you take this truth to heart.

LINGER

Psalm 139; Romans 8:31-39; Ephesians 1:13-14

RESPOND

Lord, where can I go from your presence? Where can I flee from your Spirit? For when I feel like I am losing my way, that the spiritual struggles as I wrestle through my pain will overtake me, you take me by my hand and show me where you are. You are always with me, watching me, seeing to my heart. Lord, keep coming closer. In Jesus' name, amen.

PRAISE

"Here I Am" by JWLKRS Worship with Ashley Hess

6

SPRING RAINS WITHIN

Finding God in Spiritual Dryness

HE WILL COME TO US. **HOSEA 6:3**

A drive through the Oregon desert lands me deep in a state park, looking for water. Red clay canyons curve and lead me to rocky formations that curl into the stark blue sky. Heat rises from the dirt as I step out of the Jeep and let my eyes drink in the rocks, the patches of tall grass and trees tapered through the trail. I have no idea where I am or how to get back, and the sun beats down on my already singeing skin. It's a terrible beauty, this detour into low country wilderness, slow silence spreading not only to my ears, but my soul as well.

Spiritual dryness leaves us disoriented and directionless.

How can God help us when we are unable to see him like we normally do?

We look for his handiwork. Sun on our skin, blades of grass through our toes, the blanket of blues in a Great Lake that stretches forever—they point us to his unmatched beauty, and our hearts can receive his glory from what's around.

The heavens declare the glory of God; the skies proclaim the work of his hands. Day after day they pour forth speech;

night after night they reveal knowledge.
They have no speech, they use no words; no sound is heard
from them. Yet their voice goes out into all the earth,
their words to the ends of the world.

PSALM 19:1-4

Community is key too. It is good to keep company with people who love the Lord and have gone through their own seasons of distress. Their faith is tried and true, and they can remind us of who God is and point out where he is in our lives.

Carry each other's burdens, and in this way you will
fulfill the law of Christ.

GALATIANS 6:2

And we can hold on to his Word. Though the words may not literally jump off the page, God's Word moves and is at work while we read or speak it out loud. In Scripture, we are reminded of who God is, and we can hold to truth for today to keep us steady as we grow through seasons and circumstances.

The word of God is alive and active. Sharper than any
double-edged sword, it penetrates even to dividing soul
and spirit, joints and marrow; it judges the thoughts
and attitudes of the heart.

HEBREWS 4:12

We can look for God in his handiwork, we can hear him through his people, and we can hold on to his Word through a time of spiritual dryness. This season *will* pass, and there will be a point where we see that God's presence is everywhere and we feel that our hearts are nourished and satisfied. Until then, we keep doing the next thing in front of us, surround ourselves with people who will walk this road with us, and keep inviting the Lord into this desert.

Let us acknowledge the Lord; *let us press on to acknowledge him. As surely as the sun rises, he will appear; he will come to us like the winter rains, like the spring rains that water the earth.*

HOSEA 6:3

The desert will not last. Spring rains are on the way. And while we wait for our parched places to fill again with springs of living water, we take our faith a little deeper and look at the evidence of his presence around us. He draws us deeper, sustains us on the way to those spring rains within.

REFLECT

Might God be inviting you into a new season with him that requires patience and faith in different ways? What might that be?

How can you find him with you right now? Ask God to give you eyes to see him in ways you haven't before.

LINGER

Deuteronomy 6:6-9; 2 Corinthians 5:7; 1 Peter 4:8-10

RESPOND

Lord, this season of staleness of faith is disorienting and dis-couraging. I long to hear your voice like I did before. I long for your presence, for your Spirit to be alive in me. Revive my heart, and help me see your glory in nature, your kindness through others, and your truth in your Word. You will refresh my soul again; in the meantime, let me lean on my faith in greater ways. In Jesus' name, amen.

PRAISE

"Desert Song" by Brooke Ligertwood

7

WATCHING, TRUSTING, WANTING

Awaiting Hope When We Can't Be Comforted

WATCH IN HOPE. **MICAH 7:7**

My body freezes, dread snaking through my veins. I know this feeling and never wanted to experience it again. Another anxiety attack, years after I thought I'd managed to rid myself of this panic. Soon after my body is rendered immobile, my mind spirals out of my control, spinning into crippling fear and spitting out intrusive thoughts. Between the needle-like injections of adrenaline overloading my nervous system and the deafening noise screaming in my head, my anxiety has come back with a vengeance and there is no way to calm it down. I don't see my fear ever yielding, my panic amplified by the fact that I'm still experiencing this at this point in my life. God and I worked so hard through the years, and he knows this is a place I would spare anyone from going. So why is it happening again? Fear dominates me, and all I can do is weakly call to the Lord and remind myself of his characteristics to carry me through.

Have you ever felt like you've come back from hitting rock bottom, only for life to jackhammer its surface so you can sink even deeper than you went before? In times of trial and pulsing panic, we can recite all the Bible verses we know about God's presence and help, but their comfort may still fall flat. Sometimes, the pain just doesn't go away. What then? How could God allow us to fall again? Where is he when we're faced with our darkest headspace once more? Is there an end to the pain, to the perceived disappearance of God's presence, to the unsettledness in our spirit? How do we approach the God we know and love when he doesn't take us out of our suffering?

We may not have clear-cut answers that lend immediate comfort, but as we wrestle with feeling abandoned, we remind ourselves of the truth we find in Scripture and God's promises that God is near, and we couldn't be held any closer.

God is here, protecting us, keeping us with a gentle but firm grip as he watches over us (Isaiah 41:10). He won't let go.

His hand guides us and lifts us as we sit in a hospital room, watching a loved one's heart beat on a monitor. His soothing touch is with us in those sleepless nights when yet again, the cries of our hearts and anxious minds fuse into long stretches of pacing around the house. His gaze is set upon us when betrayal rips and rends our lives into pieces.

In those sorrowful and fear-filled moments, when we wonder what our faith is about, he is ever watchful, attentive, and aware of our questions, anger, anxiety. Amid life's upheaval, as we grasp for anything that will ground us, what sustains our spiritual discontent from a soul that yearns for comfort? The trusted words of the one who has been present with us all along. Yes, even here, in the last place we'd choose to be.

As for me, I watch in hope for the LORD, *I wait for God my Savior; my God will hear me.*

MICAH 7:7

Here is where we extend our faith once more, choosing to believe that God is who he says he is, and if he has been a God who comes near to his children, he will continue to be the God who comes near to us. And so, we wait in hope for him to come. Even though hope can be hard to find, we can hold on to Hope himself because God promises he is sure and true, the one who sustains our hope in the first place (Isaiah 46:4). We don't have to believe hard enough or muster up the dregs of our faith to make him come to our aid. His presence is already here; his heart is already moved. He already does the heavy lifting, fighting for us, soothing us, holding our heads above the water, and promising we won't go under.

God is well aware of where we are and what we are going through. His ear is always open to our cries, his hand always ready to intervene on our behalf. Even when we feel trapped in a spiritual slump and wonder how we will be revived. *Especially* then.

To watch and wait in hope is to hitch our hearts once more to God our Savior, whose ear is tuned to our terrible days and unending nights as he pulls us close and offers us a precious place in his presence. God will meet us here, walking alongside us when we have no way out but through.

This is our reminder that we are more than okay, even in the moments that don't feel okay. The Lord is our way, our truth, and our life (John 14:6), and through Immanuel, God is with us, in the best and worst of it all.

REFLECT

When have you experienced fear paralyzing your faith? What might God want to say about that?

Picture Immanuel with you, his hand holding your weary heart. How can you keep this image with you today?

LINGER

Jeremiah 23:23-24; John 17:11; Hebrews 4:16

RESPOND

Oh Lord, how can something so scary come back into my life again? Sometimes I feel like I've fallen so far there's no way out. All I see is darkness and despair, a fear that terrorizes me. I can't make sense of anything. Lord, do you still see me here? Will you show me that you are also here with me, and you are making a way forward for me? Wrap me in your truth and love and remind me that you are well aware of this and working for my good. In Jesus' name, amen.

PRAISE

"Highlands (Song of Ascent)" by Benjamin William Hastings

8

THE PACE OF PEACE

Savoring Closeness with God

MY SOUL FINDS REST. **PSALM 62:1**

We can spin ourselves silly trying to reach where God already is. He can seem elusive at times, so we try to take it on our shoulders to seek him out. We expand our time in the morning to read the Bible, take more breaks in the day to say our prayers, and push through the strain of our thinking to find the right mindset to believe what he says. None of these are bad habits or goals for us to have, but we want to make sure we take a healthy approach to them. We may exhaust ourselves, stretching into a way of looking for God that just doesn't fit, when we can instead stop the searching and recognize that God is with us more than we know.

He's in the wind that refreshes us on a sweltering summer day, the cozy warmth of a blanket we pull over our knees on a winter's night. He's in the decisions we mull over and the soothing squeeze of a loved one's hand in ours. He is with us in our tired mornings when we have to drag ourselves out of bed, in the unexpected phone calls, and in the croon of our favorite song coming on the radio.

In him are all things, and by him all things hold together (Colossians 1:17).

When what we've done to get closer to God just doesn't *do it* for us any longer, it's time to let our minds rest and simply *be*.

Closeness with God isn't something to be conjured up by our own efforts; he isn't made happy when we get the timing of our quiet time just right or read a book of the Bible in one week. God is a living being, and his love is measured in his essence (1 John 4:7-8). Heart to heart, he wants us to *know* him, the way we know the wrinkled lines of our loved ones' faces or know that we rest best by the waterside. He is intimately aware of us and all our intricacies, and what he ultimately longs for is that we get to know *who he is* and choose to spend our time with him, in open conversation as with a friend, trusting him as a parent who deeply has our good in mind.

Truly my soul finds rest in God;
my salvation comes from him.

PSALM 62:1

When time with God seems stale, simply *be*. Get outside and wander among the birch trees or follow the trickle of a stream. Sway in the sweet grass and look at where he is with you in the natural wonder. *Breathe him in.*

Close your eyes. Pay attention to those breaths, the rise and fall of your chest, the soft exhale. He is in those breaths; his Spirit sustains you. He is the one who is always is coming closer; let him. Stop striving and be still (Psalm 46:10), know that he is God, the God exalted among the nations who knows your name and can never forget you (Isaiah 49:15).

Stay in step with God by staying still just a bit longer. The stagnant stretch will shift as we take the pressure off trying to meet with him the right way. There is no right way; there is only the heart posture of making room for him.

Come, be with me, Jesus beckons. Will we too relax into our Savior's embrace, just as the one Jesus loved (John 13:23) reclined into his side?

There is much he longs to share with us, a call to come closer, to hear him in an intimate place.

Call to me and I will answer you and tell you great and unsearchable things you do not know.

JEREMIAH 33:3

Pick the pace of peace. See what takes shape spiritually when you sit with him and stay close to God's heart. Can you hear him? Whispering his soothing words over your weary heart?

We get silent, slow our thoughts and trying, and wait. Wait for his presence, his movement, his voice. We go in with no expectations other than for him to show up with us.

This is where all our trying, our striving, our doing, is stripped away and we lean into the soft rest our souls long for. In him is our salvation (Romans 10:9), settling into simply being with our God who loved us first. It's not about what we do or how we do it, it's about knowing we are absolutely safe in the arms of our God, assured of his everlasting love and faithfulness to us simply because we are his children.

REFLECT

What has been your pace of life? Have you been trying to do all the right things to feel his presence?

How might God be inviting you into a pace of peace? Be still with him. Calm your mind, find a quiet place, sit down, and invite him to be with you there.

LINGER

Psalm 145:18; Ecclesiastes 7:8; Jeremiah 2:25

RESPOND

Father, I try to do all the right things to meet with you and know you are with me. I try too hard, and I miss that I can simply sit with you and be present with you. Forgive me for my chasing after the ways of being with you rather than your presence. Slow me down. May I breathe you in, be still, and pick up the pace of your peace. In Jesus' name, amen.

PRAISE

"Peace" by Josh Baldwin

INTO THE CAVERN:

INNER BATTLES

—

The lip of this rock-hewn cavern starts small, but as we enter into the gaping darkness, lit only by our lanterns, we soon come to a wide-open space the size of a small ballroom. A far-off echo of dripping water reverberates off the walls, slicking the stone below and around us. To our left, a steep decline leads deeper into the darkened cavern. Straight ahead, I shine my light over a sharp archway in the granite. From the looming echoes made by our footsteps and the cough of the cavern halls, this place has a feeling of enormity. We are afraid to take even one tiny step because we cannot see the floor beneath us.

Mental and emotional anguish are fickle foes that steal our ability to reside in the moment, to be present for the world around us. Our minds take over, faulty thinking looping unnatural patterns within us, and sometimes the buzz of static in our brains is too much to bear. We want the facts, we want assurance; we want to know: When we can't get a grip on our own reality, does God have a grip on us?

Waiting for answers is hard, often excruciating. Waiting for healing. Waiting for a dream to materialize. Waiting to hear the voice of God. *Especially* when we wonder if God is going to answer. It seems like we will never hold up living in limbo until we discern a change, no matter how subtle. When we aren't given the blueprints and are left in ambiguity, our chests tighten, our minds start spinning, and panic rises. But what if fear is actually making us stronger? What if a little dose of fear is healthy as we grow and lean into faith?

9

CLOUDS OF UNCERTAINTY

Adjusting Our Perspective

LED THROUGH THE SEA. **PSALM 77:19**

For the past few months, fear has moved into my heart and mind, stretched its limbs, and made a home where it had no invitation.

I don't think of myself as a fearful or worried person, but because of my clinical anxiety and recent seasons of setback and what-ifs, my first reactions lately have been led by fear rather than faith. I worry about the stability of my job, my health, my family, and the quality of life I want to maintain, not to mention the state of current events and the unpredictability of where things are heading. I can't seem to see my way through or work my mind out of its anxiousness. And I long for answers and timelines more than anything, so when it becomes apparent I won't be receiving them, I find myself panicking.

I think a thousand thoughts about the reasons I'm being tested, but the closer I try to get to the big picture, the less I truly see and understand. It's like my life is one big maze, and I am running around corners in search of the blue skies and fresh air that will greet me when I finally reach the exit. Yet in all this searching, never once did I expect to encounter so many rows after rows of dead ends.

So often, uncertainty seems to roll into our lives and our hearts like clouds that won't part, obscuring for too long the clarity on the other side that's fighting to break through. What about you? Where is God in this maze, in the unknown, in your searching and striving? How can this tumultuous season move our minds closer to confidence in him?

By remembering that our faith points us forward, even when little else is visible. By turning to the God who has endured with us before, and who is with us now.

Your path led through the sea, your way through
the mighty waters,
though your footprints were not seen.

PSALM 77:19

Though we may not see the footprints of God beside us on these murky mornings and dismal days, we can hold fast to his faithfulness from times before, recalling the ways he has come through for us before, especially in those seasons when we couldn't see his face.

God has seen our unformed bodies before we came into being. He has never forsaken us, nor taken his all-seeing eyes off us. Though we stumble and tumble through the clouds, we are not alone. We may not see, but we can trust. God knows our minds, along with the situations that have sent us spinning and our tendencies to doubt and waver. But he remains steady and true, reminding us of his promises to guide, provide, and sustain us while we walk through the uncertainty.

Those who know your name trust in you, for you, LORD,
have never forsaken those who seek you.

PSALM 9:10

We may never find the exact clarity we seek or fully understand why we've gone through all we have. But that's okay, because we don't *need* the answers; we just need to know the one who holds our days in his hands, who sees us when we fear and can't put a finger on exactly why. His patience with us is unending, and he loves us more than we can know.

We need to acknowledge that this time of confusion and uncertainty *will* pass. There are good times and new adventures ahead at the next turn, and we are closer to God's comfort than we may imagine. Knowing he is here now allows our peace to outweigh our fear.

May the Lord of peace himself give you peace
at all times and in every way.
The Lord be with all of you.
2 THESSALONIANS 3:16

He is here, holding us through our fear and making good on his promises to us. He is here while we discern our next turn, even when we can't see where it leads. Choosing to trust takes us deeper into the heart and faith of God, and that is the best place to be. And when the haze finally lifts, we'll realize we were never once left alone.

REFLECT

What fears have occupied your mind lately? How can you take those fears to God today?

How does knowing God is with you even in clouds of

uncertainty give you comfort? What reminds you of his presence on days that feel clouded by worry or uncertainty?

LINGER

Psalm 29:11; Romans 12:9; 1 Thessalonians 5:21

RESPOND

Father, I thank you that through all my uncertainty, questions, and confusion, you have been with me, right by my side. You know how my head and heart spin, yet you steady them with your soothing hand. Please continue to hold me close. Please walk with me as I try to navigate this maze, because I cannot even try to go at it without you. In Jesus' name, amen.

PRAISE

"Truth I'm Standing On" by Leanna Crawford

10

HOW TO UNTANGLE

Holding on Through the Unbearable

THEY CRIED TO THE LORD. **PSALM 107:19**

I wake to a new day, sleep still lingering in my eyes. As my body stirs, so does my mind. I notice, again, the weight in my chest. It's been the pattern for weeks, my constant companion in my waking hours. Frustration settles in as I prepare to battle through another day weighed down. How did anxiety and depression wind themselves so tightly within me? Sometimes, all the prayer I can whisper is, "Help."

I share this with my husband, Eric, as I brew the coffee, kettle boiling, beans ground into powder for my pour over. He takes my face in his hands and leans in close, nuzzles my nose.

"It's like a tangled fishing line," he explains. "There can be many knots—big ones that take a lot of line, and small, tight ones that seem almost impossible to sort. But you work them out, take your fingers and roll the line between them to soften the strained knot. It takes time, and you have to be patient, but eventually the knots loosen and come undone, and you've got a full, clean line again. Sometimes you have to clip the line, sometimes you lose a hook, but eventually it works out, if you take the time and care."

I stare into his blue eyes. His next words are almost a whisper. "That's what God's doing with you. You are uniquely made and it's beautiful. Something's gotten tangled inside, and he's sorting it out with his own hands, helping you untangle."

My eyes shut and I hold to his words. That's a new picture I've never drawn before: the tender process of becoming undone to be pieced back together. My insides struggling like a tangled line, taut and constricting. The fear of staying stuck makes the knots that tighten me flail even more. But then come the strong and nimble fingers of my Lord, massaging out the clump of knots crimping my life flow. Bending close, breath on my face as he studies what has curled to choke me inside, maneuvers each strand to slip free.

In Mark 5, we see a woman who suffered from bleeding reach in desperation for the hem of Jesus' robe as he passed by:

> A large crowd followed and pressed around him. And a woman was there who had been subject to bleeding for twelve years. She had suffered a great deal under the care of many doctors and had spent all she had, yet instead of getting better she grew worse. When she heard about Jesus, she came up behind him in the crowd and touched his cloak, because she thought, "If I just touch his clothes, I will be healed." Immediately her bleeding stopped and she felt in her body that she was freed from her suffering.
>
> At once Jesus realized that power had gone out from him. He turned around in the crowd and asked, "Who touched my clothes?" (verses 24-30).

Jesus turned, called her to him, then bent to see her eyes. He held her gaze, took the tangle of her broken heart, and loosened the knots of fear and shame, replacing them with the truth that she was seen, known, and loved in greater ways than she could have anticipated. And it started with her faith and belief in who Jesus was and what he could do.

He said to her, "Daughter, your faith has healed you.
Go in peace and be freed from your suffering."

MARK 5:34

We too fall at the feet of Jesus in desperation. We cry out to the Lord in our distress, and he turns to us, hearing our hearts. Our faith is built on the hope in his power to heal and that there is no knot he can't untangle, no crooked path he won't make straight (Isaiah 45:2). Here, when we're heavy and held under an oppressive fog, he reminds us that he is near, even while we struggle underneath the strain. The Lord is gracious; the Lord is strong (Isaiah 30:18). And he's never once left us to sit with the heaviness alone. It's a promise we can claim: When we cry out, he swoops in to save. We may not know his timing or ways, but we can know his character—his goodness, his faithfulness, his promise to deliver and comfort us—well enough to hold out hope that he who made us just as we are will not lose his grip.

Is this a step closer to intimacy where we find our God Immanuel, the one who wants to be with us? God, in all his mystery and love, can take our tangled mess and love us back to life. Over time, he can replace tears with joy. He can bring a fresh dose of hope to our hopeless hearts. He can tenderly remind us of his constant care in our lives. He can use the people around us to show us his love in tangible ways. If we lean in and allow him his work, we find his presence, find healing strength in him.

As the coffee steams from my cup, my hand presses Eric's strong and steady forearm. It's a moment of reprieve, resting in the love God shows through him, letting even one small knot begin the process of becoming untangled.

REFLECT

How has God come through for you before? How does this knowledge of his past provision shape how you approach him today?

Invite the Lord to come close so he can begin to untangle what's inside. Remember, his hands are gentle and skilled.

LINGER

Psalm 145:18-19; Isaiah 65:24; Jeremiah 17:14

RESPOND

Lord, I am so weary and worn down. This heaviness won't lift, and I am tired of trying to get through one day after another. You say that when I cry out to you, you hear me, and you save me in my distress. You don't lose your grip on me. Lessen my suffering with the gentle and steady comfort of your love. In Jesus' name, amen.

PRAISE

"You're Gonna Be OK" by Jenn Johnson

11

A REAL AWAKENING

Believing God Is at Work

REVIVE US AGAIN. **PSALM 85:6**

March 2022

It's too early to be up. At least *I* think so. But the gray shadowed daylight is slowly brightening, and my body keeps me up anyway, so I shuffle down the hall to the living room and lower myself to the couch. I hear the hum of cars already on the go and the bustle of early risers. My body aches, but my mind is alert. It's too early to be this revved up, but it has been the pattern for months: jitters and a racing mind, so terribly tired from fighting against anxiety and a head fog that has left me disconnected with my body and the people around me. Such is the suffering of long COVID and the trauma of yet another medical setback.

I am tired of all the physical exhaustion of my body trying to regulate itself, and of the mental exhaustion of working through patterns of fear and not knowing what's truly at the root of everything. I am tired of all the confusion that leaves me like I'm living underwater, like I am a sleepwalker longing to wake up. I long for a *real* awakening, where I am clear in mind and light in heart. Where I experience deep joy that wells up in me and bubbles out. It has been such a long winter, and the beginning of the messy spring streaks my soul with layers of heaviness and uncertainty.

For months I've raised my voice to the Lord, asking him to take away the extreme fatigue, the crippling anxiety, and complete loss of direction. Each day is enough trouble on its own. I've pleaded for the tiniest bit of relief, an escape from the strain of stress to the blessing of repose. It's been my desperate need to know that I could get through another day.

I've been spun into an unfamiliar orbit in these months of wondering how the God who says he loves me could see my suffering and sit still, observe without intervening. I've struggled to understand how a good God could stand by and watch while every inch of me suffered, physically and mentally. Every prayer became a breath suspended in wait.

We long to know the God who loves us, but we balk when he doesn't seem to relieve life's pressure. How does he move when it seems like his response is like molasses, slow, thick, and unclear?

He is here with us, even buried under the weight of our struggle. He often can do his best work while we are waiting, patiently enduring seasons of suffering. The psalmist tells us to take heart and wait on the Lord (Psalm 27:14), and God himself tells us he gives us treasures in the dark (Isaiah 45:3). Just look at the decades-long journey he took Joseph on (Genesis 37, 39–41). Even though Joseph was abandoned by his brothers, sold into slavery, falsely accused of sexual misconduct, and forced to spend years in prison, Joseph developed a character much richer than all the wealth of Egypt. He came out from his season of suffering fully dependent on God and full of wisdom and humility, and then helped lead millions through a once-in-a-lifetime famine.

Joseph faithfully endured and trusted God through the twists of his life. And in those times of uncertainty, he talked to God about his situations and set his heart on obedience to respond in faith right where he was. We can take what Joseph did, adjust our hearts, and move our lips in prayer to a new level of honesty: *Breathe in me, Lord; let your oxygen fill my lungs and revive me again. It is not enough to long for it; I ask in faith for you to move in me. In every sinew, every cell, every stem of my brain and beat of my heart. Lift me from the mire and place me on sure ground. To whom else can I go? You hold eternal life out toward me.*

The Lord will carry our fears, carry our burdens. Our deep-rooted fears of feeling unseen and abandoned will tempt us to question God and his faithfulness, but hold steady and have patience. The wait may be long, but we can lay the weight of it all on the one who holds us up and will not let us go under. Even with Joseph, God was aware of every stop he made and made a way. When Joseph was sold into slavery, God granted favor in the eyes of Pharoah's official Potiphar, who set him over his entire household. And when he was thrown in jail, Joseph oversaw the inmates and prison. God is able, always able. And always good. The Lord will keep coming after us, keep fighting for us, keep healing and growing us as he makes a way, while we make a life in him.

---

*Just as you received Christ Jesus as Lord,
continue to live your lives in him, rooted and built up in
him, strengthened in the faith as you were taught, and
overflowing with thankfulness.*

COLOSSIANS 2:6-7

Being here today means we have made it through last night. The sun always rises, even on a cloudy day. We will continue to endure, and along the way, we can find comfort and courage counting the mini victories along the way. God is growing us, inch by inch. Prayer in wait is painful, but consider the garden. Some plants actually grow best in shade or tucked in between a cluster of bushes. While we may not be able to see immediate results and grow frustrated in feeling like God doesn't see us, be assured that God indeed sees, and he is doing careful and deliberate healing work. He who sifts his hands in the soil is doing good within us. Though our destination is unseen, hold to faith that God is moving us toward beauty, blessing, and a goodness, while forging our character with a perseverance and grace that will endure.

REFLECT

What has been weighing you down? Where would you like God to meet you in your struggle? Be honest with him.

What burdens can you give to the Lord today? What, if anything, makes you hesitant to take that load off your own shoulders?

LINGER

Psalm 80:19; Isaiah 57:15; Ephesians 5:13-14

RESPOND

You are the God who calls himself good, and kind, and faithful. And you are true to your word. I am so tired and burdened;

will you lean in and come alongside me here? See me through, carry my burdens. You are always able and always good. In Jesus' name, amen.

PRAISE

"In the Morning" by JJ Heller

12

WHEN DARKNESS DESCENDS

Letting God's Love Light Our Way

A LIGHT ON MY PATH. **PSALM 119:105**

Daylight shrank as the weak winter sun disappeared, darkness stretching deep into the morning and ushered in again early in the evening. Darkness outside me; darkness inside me. My mind twisted and clouded with the scratch of a steady stream of static, rendering it nearly impossible to pay attention to the words of my family, coworkers, and friends. I descended into the abyss of anxiety and depression, pulled under the surface where nothing I did could shake the sluggish shape that was me. Even when the milky light filtered through my windows when I woke, the weight of what held me down never lifted, never offered me hope as I fought to begin and get through my day.

Sludging through the hours with my brain on fire and body beyond exhaustion, I saw no way through, no beam of light come to bring a new dawn of my heart. Only a small flicker of flame reflected in a song coming on my Spotify playlist at the precise moment I needed it, or a sentence on a page of Scripture that reminded me who God was, or the kind eyes of Eric holding me when I offered him my deepening fears of where I was headed.

But these flames turned into embers that endured, even in my darkest moments. These glimmers of God gave me enough perseverance to go on, to breathe a sigh of relief, as I collapsed into bed, that I made it through another day, and that I could hang what little, sputtering hope I had on him.

In our darkest days, the smallest speck of light can illuminate the hard-to-reach places in those of us who need a way forward.

Your word is a lamp for my feet, a light on my path.
PSALM 119:105

God doesn't blaze up the entire sky before us and divulge the entire trail. But he does offer us a lantern's length of light to let us take one step, and then another. The less that's illuminated, the more we have a chance to lean in closer to him and match strides. Sometimes our steps are tentative, unsure whether the ground where we will place our feet will hold our weight. Sometimes we're moving so quickly we can't even see where we're walking and have to trust that what we land on will keep us upright. In any case, when we look to God's Word to find true north, another inch of light is let out in front of us.

When we need the believing power of faith, letting Scripture light our way relieves the pressure we can put on ourselves when we think we need to do the work of trusting enough so our suffering will cease. God doesn't promise an immediate end to the pain, but he does promise that great purpose comes from it. And he promises his presence through the night.

> *I will praise the LORD, who counsels me;*
> *even at night my heart instructs me.*
>
> **PSALM 16:7**

Even when we're racked with fear in the deepest part of night, whether literally as we sleep or metaphorically in a dark season of soul, the Holy Spirit is at work within us to align God's truths to the places where we wrestle (John 16:13). We are not alone, even when we can't make out the way and wonder whether the light will ever shine within us again.

> *You, LORD, keep my lamp burning;*
> *my God turns my darkness into light.*
>
> **PSALM 18:28**

God's Word is guiding us, making a way where there is none and stabilizing our shaky hearts.

Glimpse the glimmers of God here with you, even when you can't imagine when the dawn will come. He is here; his Word warming your heart and mind, calling you closer and emboldening you to take a step into the shadows. His light is on your path; his peace encircles and empowers you. All you need is a glimmer of light to give you grace to go on.

REFLECT

How can you look for Jesus in a season of darkness?

Where have you seen him lighting your path like Psalm 119:105 says?

Speak God's promises out loud to remind yourself of his faithfulness. Find and write down one to three passages from Scripture that you can read out loud when you need that reassurance.

LINGER

Genesis 1:2; John 8:12; 1 John 1:5

RESPOND

God, this darkness feels heavy and unyielding. I am searching for light. Lord, illuminate my mind and heart with the power of your presence. Light the way for my next step, even if it's simply to rest in you and trust. You are my true north; you are my guiding light. I believe you will see me through. In Jesus' name, amen.

PRAISE

"Let There Be Light" by Bryan and Katie Torwalt

13

FREE ME FROM MY FEARS

Noticing God's Presence Amid Uncertainty

THE LORD REPLIED. **EXODUS 33:14**

I don't like to remember certain medical symptoms and situations I've experienced. When I think about them, fear tightens its hold around my head and chest, and I find myself worrying that if those things have happened to me, then who's to say I couldn't face another mountain to climb with my health, possibly even greater than before? I'm afraid. Even though I can logically string information together about symptoms, percentages, and odds and recognize what risks aren't likely, I am still prone to worry.

Rather than remembering the ways the Lord came through for me then and thank him for his faithfulness, I spin into situations that aren't reality and work myself up about worst-case scenarios. How can I still be so scared when I know that God's got me? If I could calm myself down and imagine him with me, what would he say?

What would God say to you amid whatever worry you're fixated on?

We all have short memories of God's goodness and grace over our difficult days, and we are prone to place doubt at the forefront when faced with something that looks and feels eerily similar to the last time. Yet even when we focus more on our what-ifs than the presence of our Savior, he is compassionate and doesn't run out of patience when we run toward our fears. He knows our human tendencies and frailties, the way our hearts beat a little faster and our minds ruminate a bit too long on a lingering unknown.

The LORD replied, "My Presence will go with you,
and I will give you rest."
EXODUS 33:14

God offers us himself, a steady presence who sees us sway in our uncertainty and gives us rest. He gives us grace to go to him yet again after we've given way to panic rather than resting in the peace of believing he is for us and has our best in mind. He is tender to our trepidation and doesn't berate us when our belief quivers. He tucks us in the crook of his arm and reassures us of his care.

My heart is glad and my tongue rejoices; my body also
will rest secure, because you will not abandon me to the
realm of the dead, nor will you let your faithful one see
decay. You make known to me the path of life; you will
fill me with joy in your presence,
with eternal pleasures at your right hand.
PSALM 16:9-11

We can come to him with our fears, no matter how rational or irrational, and trust that he takes what troubles us seriously. And he tends to us, heart to heart, smoothing our rough edges that ached to be soothed.

Piece by piece, worry by worry, he removes the root of what keeps us tense and plants his assurance skillfully in the soil of our hearts (2 Corinthians 1:18-22).

Grace. Hope. Peace. Trust. Faith. These are seeds repurposed as we let the great Gardener tend to our overgrown places. Yes, we will worry. Worry has its way of winding its way back into our lives, but when it slips in, we can hold it out to Jesus, who can take it in his capable hands and transform it into something deeper within us: a trust that stands secure in the one who has already overcome everything to bring abundant life.

Cast all your anxiety on him because he cares for you.

1 PETER 5:7

His care carries us through our fears and worries. With him, we need not be afraid. He casts our burdens, and we breathe in, exhale out, released of what tethered us too tight. His presence brings our minds and bodies rest, and our souls are safe with him.

REFLECT

What worries and fears are you holding on to? What do you think Jesus wants you to do with them?

Remember God's presence is with you, and in his presence is rest.

LINGER

Psalm 27:4; Psalm 73:28; Luke 12:25-31

RESPOND

Lord, how many times can I take all this worry on my shoulders? My mind races, running through scenarios that haven't happened yet and fearful that I'll be all alone to face them. I know you are there, but my feelings don't match my faith. I want your presence, Lord. I want the rest you promise. I hand over my burdens and anxiety to you, because you care for me. In Jesus' name, amen.

PRAISE

"Let Go" by Kory Miller

14

BETWEEN A ROCK
AND A SAFE PLACE

Allowing Ourselves to Be Still

IN QUIETNESS AND TRUST. **ISAIAH 30:15**

I wake with a jolt after waking with a jolt multiple times through the night. With this one, I can tell I'm up for good, so I shift myself upright, pull back the curtains, and pad into the kitchen to begin my coffee-making ritual.

A quick scan of my body tells me I am already tense—the twitch in my eye, tightness of chest. I'm wound tight and can feel my anxiety working itself up before I even begin the day.

This tension has been building for months, intensifying over the last few weeks. Decisions and deadlines loom, with many variables still up in the air. I'm left with much that is out of my control, and that is a place I *do not* like to be. Between the lack of control and unknown timelines, I'm in trouble as my anxiety rises.

I know I am safe. I know the things I'm waiting for aren't the biggest things in the world, but my body doesn't seem to know that. When my mind starts moving, it's an engine propeller whirring to top speed and staying in heightened intensity. I know better, but still it begins.

What's the solution? More white knuckling through the never-ending maze of work and wait and mentally making every possible scenario in my mind? No.

Surrender.

In repentance and rest is your salvation, in quietness and trust is your strength.

ISAIAH 30:15

This is what we are offered. Our salvation, our "solution," lies in quietness and rest, trusting and turning to the Lord who gives peace of mind and heart when we hand over to him the things that wind us up. And when we wind up, let us instead let down. Turn to God, who is our Redeemer and Sustainer, the mighty one who is exalted above everything else. He is our guiding light, our King, and the one who is at work over all.

When we are frayed to the point of our bodies physically manifesting how our minds have heightened, let's take a step back. Breathe. Remind our hearts how we are safe with God.

Let go. Admit you can't do it all or hold it all together. We have limits that were wired into us.

I trust in you, LORD; I say, "You are my God."
My times are in your hands.

PSALM 31:14-15

Blessed is the one who leans into the Lord when she has nothing left, when the loose ends of life lay unraveled. Let us trust in the Lord, who has given us our breath and drawn the boundary lines for us in spacious places (Psalm 16:5-6). He is our ever-present help (Psalm 46:1). He is aware of the things that stir us up.

But we don't have to fixate on what we can't figure out. We can hold fast to the one who holds all things together. We can see his kingdom come right here in the middle of the muddied mess. God is here, holding you, guiding you, strengthening you.

We can trust that he hasn't dropped us from his care; it's quite the opposite. He is our refuge and rock, our safe place, keeping us steady in the spinning. God made us; he knows the season of our lives and where the tension tends to spike. But in his quietness and rest, we can come closer to the protection and comfort of our great God. In time, he will reset and restore us, lower the anxiety, calm, and soothe. We can count on him. Trusting in his power and goodness is strength enough for today.

REFLECT

What are ways you can release the unknowns of life to God?

How can you quiet your heart to hear God's voice and rest in his presence? Take a deep breath, hold it for four seconds, and release the breath. Remind yourself that you are safe with God.

LINGER

Psalm 23; Psalm 94:19; John 14:1

RESPOND

God, my mind moves on its own sometimes, and I feel helpless to stop spinning. Lord, you know how I hold on to control, how I long to have everything laid out and ordered. But life does not work this way. There is mystery, there is faith. Help me rest in your ever-present help and love. Quiet me with your love and let me live in the rest and trust you give. In Jesus' name, amen.

PRAISE

"Save Me" by Steffany Gretzinger

15

REFINED THROUGH FIRE

Finding God in the Flames

CONSIDER IT PURE JOY. **JAMES 1:2**

We don't like the unknown, the unanswerable. Neat, orderly, and organized is how we prefer life, thank you. I know I don't like not knowing the outcome, and if I have numerous variables to try to piece together for a decision, I'm panicked and paralyzed. I don't want to get it wrong. I don't want to let God down. I want to know which choice to make and whether it's part of God's plan for me. And when I catch the questions on loop, I work myself up to the point where my body breaks down, tightens with the tenseness, and my adrenal glands are working overtime. The pace of my life isn't sustainable, and I feel I can't even slow down to be with the Lord and hear from him, which is one of my favorite things in the entire world.

Even when we are safe, even when we know that things aren't terrible and our hardships will end, our bodies still react. They can't help but respond to the overworking of our minds and the situations we are in. Even if what we are facing now is not the same as what sent us reeling the last time, our nervous systems, when overloaded, still respond.

We may wonder why we are going through this another time—haven't we already fought the good fight of faith over this (1 Timothy 6:12)? Why do we need to go through this setback *again*? We *will* endure this, but the timeline on *when* it will end can tear us apart if we let it.

Consider it pure joy, my brothers and sisters,
whenever you face trials of many kinds, because you know
that the testing of your faith produces perseverance.
Let perseverance finish its work so that you may be mature
and complete, not lacking anything.

JAMES 1:2-4

Wait, so we are to consider our trials with *joy*? When we go through another challenge, and our bodies and minds react the same as the last time, our hearts should fill with *joy*?

Yet we are to look past the terrible to the transformation. God is allowing us to repeat a discomforting piece of our history because there is more to refine within our faith. The testing of our faith, like refiner's fire, purifies our motives, spotlights any points of weakness within our faith, and bolsters us to believe God more deeply in the midst of trial. Faith produces perseverance, which endures and strengthens us even when we may appear at our weakest.

There is purpose in this pain. The setbacks may actually be starting points that point us in a direction of greater gain in the spiritual realm. God is after our hearts, refining our faith to maturity. As we endure suffering, unknowns, and the tricky means of our minds, our inner being is being strengthened and polished to shine with the light and wisdom of Christ (2 Corinthians 4:16). We are being renewed in the refining.

God is not giving us this challenge to see whether we will fail. His grace is sufficient through the thorns of trial (2 Corinthians 12:9), to smooth our rough edges and water the places within us still stiff with a need for spiritual molding.

We get to go at it again with God alongside us. For greater is he who is in us (1 John 4:4), sharpening and shaping our souls to not only withstand temptation, trembling, and tears, but flourish in our faith, until it is mature and complete, lacking nothing (James 1:4).

Our bodies and minds will once again relax in time. In his shepherding he will guard us and direct us to not merely survive, but sustain with the strength of his power at work in us. Jesus will guide us through the fire and see our faith rise through the flames of trial.

The LORD is my shepherd, I lack nothing. He makes me lie down in green pastures, he leads me beside quiet waters, he refreshes my soul.

PSALM 23:1-3

REFLECT

What trials have you faced before that you are currently facing again? How might you see God refining your faith through these recurring battles?

How would it help you persevere if you reframed your perspective to see Jesus with you in the fire of these trials?

LINGER

Romans 5:3-5; James 1:12; 1 Peter 5:10

RESPOND

Father, again, the worry comes to me, unbidden. My body reacts to the stress and trial that I can't seem to get past. How long must I endure and go through this stretch again? Lord, reframe my heart to see how trials are good for my soul, and that you are building up my faith through my inability to see a clear way through. Guide me, my Good Shepherd. In Jesus' name, amen.

PRAISE

"Another in the Fire" by the Worship Initiative

16

AN UNEXPECTED BLOOM

Journeying into Healing

THE WILDERNESS WILL REJOICE. **ISAIAH 35:1**

There's a small orchid plant sitting snug in its base by our kitchen sink, and my husband keeps pointing out to me the slow progress it's made over the winter weeks. What started as five green buds tightly shut has transformed slowly over the course of time, opening into a beautiful arrangement of white flowers with delicate pink centers. Each time he noticed the emergence of a new bloom, Eric would call my attention to the plump bud, its small shoots of petals beginning to pull apart, and tell me to take notice over the next few days for the bloom that would soon arrive. And so I would watch. Pay attention. Notice the shift, the slow unfurling, the beauty coming into itself despite existing in a barren season when it seems like nothing will grow again. Watching the orchid has been a thing of beauty, an opportunity to keep discovering the everyday miracle of growth.

The thing is, I've been struggling with crippling anxiety again over these last few months. I've slogged through the days and nights, battling against my mind as I gripped tightly to the truth of God's Word and the evidence around me that things are okay. I've needed these petals blossoming in the bleak winter to remind me that like these little buds, I too am coming into something good.

When it comes to our healing, this is the way it often is. Healing is often slow, even imperceptible. We are caught off guard when the weeks pass and then we suddenly realize we are better off than we were in the days before. While sometimes healing *can* happen overnight, we're more familiar with a steady, ordinary deliverance that gradually makes our ailments feel like less of an emergency as our recovery emerges into something solid that we can take hold of in our hearts.

We watch and wait and notice the small changes.

In my healing journeys, I've noticed a few things:

1. Healing Takes Time

There is a time for everything, and a season for every activity under the heavens: a time to be born and a time to die, a time to plant and a time to uproot, a time to kill and a time to heal, a time to tear down and a time to build.

ECCLESIASTES 3:1-3

Like the orchid coming into bloom, God often accomplishes his work on an organic, day-by-day timeline. Healing and growth don't happen all at once. Many times, we are unable to notice their effects until we observe that something is different—we find that we have a little more energy, or our thoughts seem a bit clearer, or we have been able to get some good work in without feeling overwhelmed.

2. Healing Is Not Linear

He heals the brokenhearted and binds up their wounds.

PSALM 147:3

Healing is not a continual upward trajectory. Some days will feel like setbacks. But in the wide scope of your journey forward, look at the whole, not just the microscopic. Our faith is like this too. Decline and ascent, doubt and belief, worry and wisdom—duality weaves within the waiting, the living. If you feel more down one day, this doesn't erase the progress you've made.

3. Healing Happens in Ways We May Not Be Expecting

"My thoughts are not your thoughts, neither are your ways my ways," declares the Lord. "As the heavens are higher than the earth, so are my ways higher than your ways and my thoughts than your thoughts."

ISAIAH 55:8-9

What does healing look like to you? What do you want it to be? Perhaps a little bit of whatever has ailed you is still lingering, but resilience has built as well. If we're looking to be 100 percent normal, recovered from where we were before our injury, setback, or trial, we may need to switch our perspective to see what God is doing in the here and now. We won't be the same as we were, because we naturally progress and grow throughout our lives. And in this next season of healing, we hold to the small progressions we make through the days and weeks. We look at things in a different way. Our idea of normal may be different from what it was before. Look at where God has brought you, look at his presence and hand in your life, and lean into it. Healing is happening, though the way it looks may surprise you.

Whatever your journey, here's the core of it: Healing points to the Healer.

Ultimately, this is where our hearts land if we search the suffering and seek to dig to its root. God, our Healer, is our anchor, our sunlight, our reminder of what—or who—matters.

No matter what healing looks like, God is in the middle of it all. Because external healing aside, the internal healing within our hearts, our faith, is what he is most after. He wants us to reassess our incorrect or incomplete beliefs about him, to notice where our fears have overridden our faith, to remember the truth of his character that hasn't changed. He wants to redirect the compass of our hearts.

The desert and the parched land will be glad; the wilderness will rejoice and blossom.
Like the crocus, it will burst into bloom; it will rejoice greatly and shout for joy.

ISAIAH 35:1-2

Right now, our kitchen sink orchid is in full bloom, its wide-open white petals stretching from its branches. One green bud still waits to unfurl, but it's a little softer and looser than it was yesterday. Perhaps it will open within the week. I keep waiting, watching, knowing one morning I'll be moving around the kitchen making coffee and waking up, and my eyes will settle on the orchid and marvel at the presence of a new white bloom as the flower does what it is designed to do.

We are all doing what he has designed us to do.

REFLECT

What does healing look like for you right now? How might you begin to see more of God in the healing process?

How can looking back on how God has met you in previous situations encourage you to keep believing that he is at work in your current situation?

LINGER

Jeremiah 33:6; Joel 2:23; Zechariah 10:1

RESPOND

Father, I am tired on this healing journey. Sometimes, it feels like I am not making any progress. But remind me that you are the Healer who brings growth and recovery in unexpected ways, and that this is a process, not a one-time event. You are strong, you are steady, and you are doing a good work within me. I'm trusting you for my healing. In Jesus' name, amen.

PRAISE

"Carry" by Elias Drummer

DOWN THE RAPIDS:

SITUATIONAL STRUGGLES

———

Bumps of water strengthen into waves, and the current stretches faster the farther we move down the river. Its mouth widens as we head from tranquil to a little more tumultuous, the sway of our boat shifting between each wave. Up ahead, ribbons of white waves bob and jet among the current. Water splashes over our arms, faces, into the boat as we dip and turn. How have we not capsized? In a split second, the waters have become a raging river, rapids fiercely hurling us forward. Trees and brush on the bank blur in our vision as we slide around the bend. Panic rises; we don't know where this ends, or how, and we can't predict the next move. We're helpless, and it's a horrible feeling. Roars of water reverberate in our ears, white noise that does nothing to help calm the fear practically jumping from our hearts. How will this end?

Disappointment catches our spirit, grabs hold of its fabric and clings, tears, and knots us up. How many seasons have we thrown our hearts into the hopes of something dear to our dreams, only to see closed doors deflate us and tempt us to curl our fists around our tender hopes and hide them away?

When we're thrust into situations we didn't want to face, fear may take over, but it doesn't have control. God hands us a paddle and directs us through the twists and turns.

God knows the depths of our fears, the spoken and unspoken. And there is a way forward, even when we feel swept along in life's too-quick current. There is power in proclaiming truth among lies. There is no place too terrifying that God has not already gone to get to us.

17

DOESN'T HE KNOW I'M HURTING?

Waiting on Unanswered Prayers

THE RIGHTEOUS WILL CRY OUT. **PSALM 34:17**

I hold my breath as I click the message that just showed up in my inbox, but the air pushes out of my lungs soon after I begin to read. Another rejection to a writing project I poured my heart into. I took careful consideration with every word I put on the page and believed that maybe this was the time of longing fulfilled to a long-dreamed desire of my heart. My heart is unable to hold the disappointment together, and hot tears pool at the edges of my eyes.

Enough, I think. *Enough trying, enough putting myself out there in hope only to be let down and rejected. My heart can't take it anymore.*

Sometimes, we cry out to God and the echo of our prayer lingers a little too long without an answer, until an answer comes that appears callous. Doesn't he know we're hurting?

A dear friend receives a diagnosis no one expected. A relationship deteriorates, and there doesn't seem to be a way to stop the crumbling. A hope for a home or family haunts us as the calendar turns to another year, and still there doesn't seem to be a change on the horizon.

Waiting for answers to prayer is hard, often excruciating. But it's especially hard to grapple with when God *does* respond, but not in the way we had hoped. Sometimes, we pray and pray, and hope and trust, and the answer is simply, "No." What then? How do we still hold our hearts out to a God who didn't give us what we asked?

We may be tempted to wonder if we didn't pray correctly or ask in the right way. We may even go as far as wonder whether we had enough faith. Surely, if we loved the Lord enough, he would have answered how we had hoped. After all, according to his Word, he hears every cry of his children and turns his ear toward them (Psalm 34:17). He is always in relationship and communication with us; either we aren't tuned in to hear him or he's answering in a way we aren't expecting.

We can't fathom the ways of God. His thoughts are not like ours, nor are his ways like ours (Isaiah 55:8-9). So, what can we hold to when his answer doesn't make sense to us? When our loved one *doesn't* get better, our own illness lingers, or we just can't keep hold of a steady job? How do we have the faith to endure?

Let's shift the perspective from our lens to the lens of the Lord. As we discover that his ways are not like ours, let's trust for a moment that he does have a bigger picture in mind, and your broken heart is a part of it.

God has made his covenant with his people, and that includes communion and a promise to sustain:

> The righteous cry out, and the LORD hears them; he delivers them from all their troubles. The LORD is close to the brokenhearted and saves those who are crushed in spirit (Psalm 34:17-18).

Thank the Lord he has promised to be with us when our spirits sink and our hearts are bent. When we pray, he is aware, the Holy Spirit interceding with words we cannot humanly express.

We cry, "Where are you in this, Lord? Why won't the hurting stop?" He responds, "I'm right here, dear one. I am hurting with you."

If ever there was an example of God answering no, it was Jesus in the garden of Gethsemane, about to experience the most horrendous betrayal, beating, and crucifixion. He knew what was coming, yet being fully human, he did not want to experience it. He asked multiple times for another way, but God didn't give one. Jesus, a man of sorrows well acquainted with grief (Isaiah 53:3), reminds us that we are never alone, no matter how pressing the pain of our prayer is, or the answer that follows. In Gethsemane, as the cross loomed before him, his body and spirit quaked at what would come.

> Jesus went out as usual to the Mount of Olives, and his disciples followed him. On reaching the place, he said to them, "Pray that you will not fall into temptation." He withdrew about a stone's throw beyond them, knelt down and prayed, "Father, if you are willing, take this cup from me; yet not my will, but yours be done." An angel from heaven appeared to him and strengthened him. And being in anguish, he prayed more earnestly, and his sweat was like drops of blood falling to the ground (Luke 22:39-44).

Jesus, who was welcomed mere days earlier to Jerusalem and hailed as Savior, carried the crushing weight of being wrongfully accused, struck down, and sentenced to die. Here in the garden in the quiet of the night, he came to his Father, fully aware of the situation, begging for another way. Yes, he wrapped up his plea with "Thy will be done," but that didn't stop his stress. Blood dripped from his forehead instead of sweat as he poured out his fear to his Father. He was making one last plea for another way, yet there was no other way. Jesus accepted this and responded with obedience and strength that could only come from God.

Jesus empathizes with us in the middle of our pain.

The way out is often through. But a good God walks with us through suffering, guides us when we don't know what to do. We endure, build our spiritual muscles, and grow a perseverant faith that builds when we remember the ways God has answered our prayers before.

Have you questioned whether God has heard the cry of your heart? Have you held out a hope that flickers, a fledgling prayer birthed from your own burden or the pain of someone else? Do you waver and wonder what he genuinely thinks of you, to hold off on responding to such a sensitive and personal plea?

Hear this: Your God's ears are always tuned to your voice. His eyes are ever upon the plight of his people (Exodus 2:25), the little one in ICU, the couple existing in one house yet in separate lives, the growing fear in not finding work week after week.

Believe he doesn't miss a thing. Believe he is faithfully working on your behalf. And above all, believe his heart toward you is good and full of love.

REFLECT

Have you been praying for something for a long time and haven't yet received an answer? How has this impacted your approach to prayer?

How can you still hold your heart out to God and hope while you wait for him to respond? Share with him any feelings of disappointment or frustration you're experiencing as you continue to be vulnerable with him in prayer.

LINGER

Isaiah 40:28-31; Isaiah 53:1-6; James 5:7-8

RESPOND

Lord, you do not miss a thing. You are attentive, you take care, and you are never late with your timing. Forgive me when I panic when things don't seem to go according to how I'd like. Replace my panic with peace as you fill me with your presence in the meantime. In Jesus' name, amen.

PRAISE

"Christ the Lord Is With Me" by Steffany Gretzinger

18

A HOLE IN MY HEART

Letting God Tend to Our Wounds

HE HEALS THE BROKENHEARTED. **PSALM 147:3**

August 2019

The doctor breezes into the square taupe examining room, an iPad in his hand. His eyes explore the screen before lifting and finding mine. "Your heart looks good," he says, nodding. I let go of the breath I didn't know I was holding.

My heart wasn't always good. A year prior, I was thrown off guard when I suffered a stroke at age 33. I couldn't believe it. My shock spiraled further when that stroke led to the discovery that I had a patent foramen ovale: a hole in my heart. Where the chambers meet, they never closed, allowing blood clots to sneak their way out of the chambers and into other places in my body where they should not be, like my brain. It was something I was born with; the hole should have closed when I was a baby, but it never did. And while I had surgery to close the hole and have recovered just fine, it still shocks me that I went all my life with it and I didn't know. I was a college athlete and had run half marathons, and all that time, nothing had happened, yet I had been a ticking bomb waiting to burst.

We are all ticking down our days, waiting with wounds, wondering if we will burst. You may wrestle with your physical health—recovery from surgery that feels endless, an ongoing illness you can't shake off, lingering pain that doctors don't have answers for—that leave you in limbo, exhausted and challenged each day to find fresh hope. It can be hard, so hard, to believe things can get better while sitting in the unknown.

How long, LORD? Will you forget me forever? How long will you hide your face from me? How long must I wrestle with my thoughts and day after day have sorrow in my heart? How long will my enemy triumph over me?

PSALM 13:1-2

You may wrestle with your own struggles—situations that seem to stay stuck, no matter how much praying and thinking about how to best bring about resolutions. That too gets tiring.

Whatever the pain, wherever you are, God wants to fill the holes in our hearts. Mine were literal, but I had the metaphorical ones too. We all do—a hole of not feeling good enough. Of being let down by a trusted friend, a confidence shattered. Of the disappointment of crushed dreams. Of the absence of a parent, either during our formative years or later in life—you name it, the brokenness of life creates rifts in our hearts that we long to have fixed.

Jesus, the lover of our souls, went to the cross to fill the gap for us (1 Peter 2:24). But he first came to earth to experience the weight of emotions that come with living this life, so we would know that he understands exactly what we are experiencing. Yes, we are hurting, recoiling against the pain. But he holds us as we endure the pain, and he loves us too much to just leave us where we are.

There is healing for you. There is healing for me. God wants to close the holes in us and restore us.

He heals the brokenhearted and binds up their wounds.

PSALM 147:3

Our God is close to the brokenhearted—that's us. But first, we must take our hands off those holes and allow him access. We have been protecting ourselves from pain, but blocking the actual core of the problem prevents the beginning of our restoration. He wants to work with us through a healing journey, but he won't force himself into our pain. It has to be our decision, our invitation to him.

But when we do invite him into those deep places of our hearts, he takes our wounds and cleans them, rubs gently—though it may sting—and cauterizes them to cure any infection. We are given the best care possible to make a full and satisfying recovery. So our hearts are as good as new. So we may no longer endure surviving but find a way to *thrive*.

He not only wants to take away that emptiness, but he wants to fill us up with all he offers.

May the God of hope fill you with all joy and peace as you trust in him, so that you may overflow with hope by the power of the Holy Spirit.

ROMANS 15:13

God can and *will* fill us with joy, peace, and hope, so our whole-ness can bear witness to our healer God.

We need to let him in. Uncurl your fists, let your heart lay exposed, and let God's sure and steady hands do the good work of binding your wounds, healing your heart, and filling you with his deep and over-flowing hope.

There is beautiful healing work to be done in our hearts, once we give God access. His intention is to heal, and he is more than willing to start right now. Open your heart and let him begin to fill what's long lain empty.

REFLECT

Where are the holes in your heart? How have you tried to fill them on your own?

Will you let God access to your pain? Feel free to tell him about your hesitations, and then dare to let him do his work.

LINGER

Psalm 147; Jeremiah 17:14; Romans 5:5

RESPOND

Father, I have hurts and holes in me that I long to have healed. I've been dismayed, I've felt alone, and I've held onto this pain on my own for far too long. Will you come into this hole and heal me? Please fill me with joy, peace, hope, and your love so I may live in the overflow you give. Thank you for being the one who binds up our wounds. In Jesus' name, amen.

PRAISE

"Healing Is in Your Hands" by Christy Nockels

19

COURAGE IN THE STORM

Finding Peace When We Feel Helpless

BUFFETED BY THE WAVES. **MATTHEW 14:24**

Some days are storms. Sometimes the storm strikes suddenly, with an unexpected and unwanted occurrence that turns our plans—and maybe even our lives—upside down. Sometimes we can see the storm on the horizon long before it arrives, a forecast-fulfilling downpour of busyness, stress, and exhaustion that leaves us stuck in this squall. But no matter the type, these storms leave us longing for control that we can't find amid the violent waves that toss us down. Our spiritual boats grow battered, pulled far from the safety of the shore as we're pushed into the danger of deeper waters.

We can feel absolutely helpless in these storms, as if one more wave will knock us out of the boat and into the water. We can grow frantic and afraid, wondering if we've been forgotten, at once desperate and hopeless as we question whether help will come.

But somewhere in the mist and moonlight, a figure appears. Moving *toward* us, on *top* of the waves. As if nothing distresses him. His eyes are fixed on our floundering boat, his hand reaching toward us. Who *is* this man who faces the swelling water and sheets of rain and does not falter?

In Matthew 14:22-33, we find Jesus' disciples separated from him and caught in a boat on in the middle of a lake, facing very literal waves and wind. The disciples are already facing trouble when, across the lake, they realize that a person—Jesus—is walking over the water toward them, and at this, they are terrified.

But Jesus sees and responds to their fears, and to ours. "Take courage! It is I," Jesus tells his disciples (and us) in Matthew 14:27. "Don't be afraid."

Jesus has come for us. His steps are steady, purposeful, sure. He knows exactly where we are in these storms, and he will stop at nothing to see us through.

The winds of struggle may blow straight at us, fierce and menacing. But Jesus walks straight toward us, striding above whatever it is we fear.

There is nothing we can't face when the Lord who can still the very waters he created sets his sights on stilling whatever storms rage around and within us. He comes to be *with us*, Immanuel, entering into our trials without hesitation (Isaiah 7:14). This is who he is. This is what he does.

He even welcomes us to step out of the boat and onto the waves with him, in direct opposition to our hearts' terror, just as he does with Peter in Matthew 14:29. He invites us with one simple word: "Come."

Here, we have the chance to let our faith be bigger than our fear, to walk toward the one who came to meet us, who stands with his hands outstretched. The God who walks on water to meet us will not respond to our trust by allowing us to sink. He wants to see our faith; he values it despite our fears, and when we face doubts, he stays near to assuage them.

Do we believe he is willing to walk into our storm, into the waves that roil against us? Do we trust him enough that when he extends the invitation to come onto the water with him, we step outside of the boat in faith?

Our faith buoys us against the storm. And if our fears overwhelm our faith just as fear overwhelmed Peter, Jesus is still waiting to catch us (Matthew 14:31). We are safe in his arms.

God directs our steps and makes them secure (Proverbs 16:9). We don't have to worry about where we're going because we know *who* guides us. It's okay to admit when we're afraid or out of our element, because God wants to hear our hearts' cries. He wants to comfort, encourage, and strengthen us through our times of struggles; he longs to show us his graciousness (Isaiah 30:18).

The more out of sorts we feel, the more we can lean into God, who has given us all we need for the journey. He walks toward us in the storm that surrounds us, so let's let Jesus calm the seas within us.

REFLECT

How have you experienced God meeting you in the middle of your storms? How have you witnessed God meet your loved ones in times of crisis? How does it comfort you to know that he is with you in your current trials?

Where and how in your current storm can you take a step of faith and come toward him in trust?

LINGER

Psalm 107:29; Proverbs 10:25; Luke 8:24

RESPOND

Father, my heart is aching today. The storms of life are tossing me about, and I am afraid and weary. Stretch my faith today through the comfort of your presence. You do not leave me; instead, you come toward me. Thank you for being in control of my life; I know I can trust you. In Jesus' name, amen.

PRAISE

"Take Courage" by Kristene DiMarco

20

SOMETHING DEEPER GROWS

Forging Faith Through Struggle

WHAT WE DO NOT SEE. **HEBREWS 11:1**

Life comes for us swiftly and without mercy—and often we get caught up in the undertow, left in situations we never saw coming and helpless to find a way out. Family members get sick, *we* get sick, we lose our jobs, we lose the ones we love, the list goes on.

How many times can we endure the same struggle? How many nights can be spent in sorrow, questions, and battered hope? Where in all of this can we see God's hand, and believe that there is more than what we can see right now?

Perhaps, in the heavy vest of hurt laid across our chests, something deeper is anchoring us. Perhaps these lopsided situations are presenting us with a chance for greater faith, a deeper sense of God and who he is to us. Something that will last and mean more than it has before.

Take heart, weary one. God is doing deep work during the dark, in these places of struggle where you wish you didn't have to go. But he is in the valley with you, walking ahead and clearing the path, stepping back to walk with you as you press on. In the deep places, the caverns and clearings, he is doing a greater work within. He is bolstering your faith, cementing what you know and believe about him to be true into the foundation of your soul, so when the next trial comes, you will stand firmer, stronger, more assured.

Faith is confidence in what we hope for and assurance about what we do not see.

HEBREWS 11:1

Your faith is being built brick by brick. This process isn't easy—quite often it can be painful and something we don't want to endure, but God often doesn't choose the quick fix. He's after deep, anchoring, transformational healing and growth. He knows what is good for us, and he knows what is needed to get us there. This is hard; this is the narrow path. But what is being produced far outweighs the effort.

Sometimes the situations we go through are collateral damage from living in a fallen world. God never wanted harm to come to you, but he will make something good grow from the difficult parts of your story (Genesis 50:20). He is forging a faith that stands solid in the face of opposition so when trouble arrives—and it *will* arrive—you know that you know that you know who the Lord is and what promises to stand on. The more certain we are of who God is in the midst of uncertainty, the more we can anchor to our true foundation and keep our footing when the earth beneath us seems to move.

Who is God? He is merciful and mighty, faithful and forever. His heart is good, and he is just, and so much more.

The LORD, the LORD God, merciful and gracious, long-suffering, and abounding in goodness and truth, keeping mercy for thousands, forgiving iniquity and transgression

and sin, by no means clearing the guilty, visiting the
iniquity of the fathers upon the children and the children's
children to the third and the fourth generation.

EXODUS 34:6-7 NKJV

Faith is being certain of what we hope for, positive of what we do not see. Often, our hope *becomes* seen as we act on our faith, grab hold of the hope in him whose character is good and loving. And our good God reaches out his hands, encouraging us on as we step on shaky feet and exercise our faith, digest his Word, and let it settle and spread in our hearts and minds.

Lean into the Lord. He hasn't left you or stepped away for a moment. He's here, looking after you. And like the good Father he is, he brings you through difficult situations to strengthen your faith for the long run. Every challenge, every hurt, every hope turned sideways—he's well aware of where these hardships have led you and the pain that has followed. He sees you in it, and he sees who you will become.

Here is where we hold to hope as our faith is developed and solidified. Faith is a certainty in what we can't see, founded on what we believe. We can trust God to take us through the tough places. We can hold to the hope we profess because he who promises is faithful (Hebrews 10:23).

REFLECT

How can God use the hard things of your story for his glory?

Where can you ask God to grow your faith today?

LINGER

Hebrews 10:23; Hebrews 11:6; 2 Corinthians 4:17

RESPOND

Lord, I never expected to experience the struggles I have endured. I am still enduring today, but I choose to believe you are at work growing good faith in me. Build me up so I am confident in who you are and can hold to your truth, for my good and your glory. In Jesus' name, amen.

PRAISE

"Braver Still" by JJ Heller

21

BRIGHTER DAYS AHEAD

Swapping Worry for Trust

MUCH MORE VALUABLE. **MATTHEW 6:26**

It's early January and there's a bird chirping outside my window. Spring is still a ways away, so what kind of bird could this be? Is it a winter bird, one that braves the unyielding cold? Or is it simply a bird that got turned around and lost her way south?

I cross the room to find out. Two plump little brown birds nestle in the branches of my lilac bush, sitting there as if all is right in the world. Do they know there is still snow and ice and frigid temperatures to come? How are they singing? How are they sitting in this bush so content and carefree? These little snowbirds don't seem to mind their surroundings, but this shouldn't come as a surprise.

> Look at the birds of the air; they do not sow or reap or store away in barns, and yet your heavenly Father feeds them. Are you not much more valuable than they? (Matthew 6:26).

These birds need not worry about the elements or season—they are provided for. Surely if these tiny birds can find a reprieve to this winter, our weary hearts can too.

What's keeping you tied up in uncertainty? The strain of your

finances, wondering how you can make one more month? Or a relationship gone sour that's left you standing in the aftermath wondering how things got so tangled? Perhaps it's the constant unknown of a
lingering illness that sets you back yet again in your week. The strain
can be too much, but keep faith. If this is a season that's dragged on
and left you longing for brighter days, do not fear. Hope is coming;
it is already here. You are seen, and you are cared for. Our God sees
to it. He has come for you.

Why do we worry about this winter in our hearts when we have
a good God watching out for us? These singing birds remind us that
spring will come again. This beacon of hope in the midst of our barren winter implores us to lift our hearts to him who takes care of the
birds. How much more are we tucked into his care?

Consider he who spared *nothing*—including his Son—to save us so
we could be made righteous and call God friend. God knows exactly
why your heart hangs heavy today, how you ache, how you question
all the things yet unknown. How will he provide? How will he come
through? Relax, breathe, remember: He is already making a way.

---

*He who did not spare his own Son, but gave him up for
us all—how will he not also, along with him,
graciously give us all things?*

ROMANS 8:32

It may be a season you can hardly stand, but you are *standing*, and
you are sustained. God has seen to that. Never has he left or forsaken
you (Deuteronomy 31:6); he is always making a way.

Look and listen out your window for the light, sweet song of the sparrow. Notice God's attention to the details of your life and how he will not let you down. Keep holding on to him, keep clinging to his promises. You are of great value to our great God; spring will come again, but he is also making a new way in your heart right now. Trust him. Let his love console you. Hitch your hope to his heart and dare to sing your own winter song of praise to warm your faith. Seek his kingdom, already coming, already here. God is a God of hope, a harbinger of spring and softer days, an anchor of strength in the here and now. He is taking care of you; you are safe with him. We are always safe with him.

REFLECT

What memories come to mind when you recall how God has provided for you in the past?

What helps you remember God's presence and faithfulness today? Tell him your needs and take a moment to really trust that he will see you through.

LINGER

Matthew 6:25-34; Luke 12:22-31; Philippians 4:19

RESPOND

Father, I'm tired and stretched thin again. I worry, I over-think, I have trouble sleeping because I'm so caught up in the unknown of my situation. But you tell me that you take care of me, that you provide for me and see me through. You promise

there will be light and life on the other side of this season,
but that you are also with me here in the middle of the hard.
Thank you for taking care of me and showing me that you are
here. In Jesus' name, amen.

PRAISE

"Jireh" by Maverick City Music

22

OUT OF CONTROL

Resting in God's Power

I WILL HELP YOU. **ISAIAH 41:13**

November 2021

I'm half-sitting, half-lying in a stiff, plastic-feeling faux leather chair in a small room with no windows scrunched in an older wing of the hospital that isn't often used. But the COVID-19 pandemic is still ongoing, and all old areas of medical wings have been resurrected to maximize space.

I'm groggy, but my bleary eyes don't leave the bed beside me where Eric stirs restlessly, hooked up to monitors; meanwhile, the in and out of nurses feeds into fears I don't like to entertain about my husband. I look at the time on my phone, and the bright numbers displayed leave me to wonder if I've actually slept at all. The hours have seemed to drag since Eric and I walked through the emergency room doors the evening before. That night at dinner, his pacemaker had chirped a warning, notifying us of a heart irregularity. This new medical emergency was arriving on the heels of a hospital stay from weeks before when he battled COVID-19 and pneumonia. Now Eric has been admitted for a heart arrhythmia, his doctors seeking to get his heart to beat on the right rhythm again. So for the time being, we're here, into this corner corridor, one of just a handful of rooms left unoccupied.

Once the nurse finds no change to his heart and Eric fades into a mild sleep, I slip out the door to pace the corridor. No one else is moving around at this hour, and the rooms I pass are quiet. I look out the windows of the glass hallway leading to another wing, restless, exhausted, completely at the end of myself. I have nothing to pray except the same few lines over again.

When was the last time you felt weary when you endured what was out of your control? It can be disorienting, the not knowing, the overload and uncertainty on all levels as you try to piece incoming information together but don't have enough comfort and answers. Where is God when we feel abandoned, when we feel as if everything has cracked and crashed out of our hands, when we just don't think we can take anymore?

There is no easy way forward but through, among the beeping monitors, in the shallow breath of the ones dearest to us, the panic pushed deep down and the sobs that can no longer be held in. Here in the depths of our despair and doubts, God bends close to pull us into himself, brushes the burden off our hearts and gives us his care instead.

When we don't know how we can hold on, here's what we can hold *to*:

> I am the LORD your God who takes hold of your right hand
> and says to you, Do not fear; I will help you (Isaiah 41:13).

God has you. Never has he taken his eyes off you, and he isn't going to start now. God's grip is secure, assuring, and will lead you safely to where you need to go.

The virgin will conceive and give birth to a son,
and they will call him Immanuel
(which means "God with us").

MATTHEW 1:23

God will be with us. Even when we feel like we have been left to face uncertainty alone, we are never by ourselves. Jesus isn't called Immanuel because it's a beautiful-sounding name; he's called Immanuel because it means *God with us*. It's reassuring that the God of the universe is so in tune with your suffering that he made a way to be even closer to you.

The LORD is with me; he is my helper.
I look in triumph on my enemies.

PSALM 118:7

God is our helper. He comes to us in times of trouble with a deep desire to help us. His heart is for you, always. And he is more than willing to take up what keeps you up at night and exchange it for his peace and comfort.

I make my way back to Eric's room where his heart still hasn't made enough progress on its own to rectify the arrhythmia, but when I settle back into that semi-recliner, I am confident that God is here in this room with us, that he has never left. He holds us all, he is with us, and he is our helper. There is relief in this knowing, which gives us just enough to hold on to as we endure another hour, another day.

REFLECT

Where are you struggling to believe God will help you right now?

How can you take heart knowing God is for and with you? Memorize Isaiah 41:13 to remind yourself of God's help and care.

LINGER

Psalm 91:4; John 1:14; 1 John 4:4

RESPOND

Father, I am at the end of myself. I am worried and feel helpless. My mind runs with anxious thoughts and fears of the unknown. I do not know what to do, but I know you do. Would you help me trust you when I am afraid? Help me look for your presence in my life as I walk through this hard thing, so I may grow closer to you in the middle of all this. Do it for the glory of your name. In Jesus' name, amen.

PRAISE

"You're Not Finished Yet" by the Belonging Co. featuring Natalie Grant

23

TRUE RADIANCE

Returning Our Focus to God

GUIDE YOU ALWAYS. **ISAIAH 58:11**

One Saturday afternoon in early fall, I decided to explore a forest near my house. I had been meaning to venture out for a while but hadn't yet made the time. I parked my car and started on a wide path covered with scattered leaves, where towering birch and oak trees surrounded me, their leaves the most vibrant yellows and soft greens.

A little way in, I came across a pile of large logs stretching over a small clearing. After looking them over, I found a sturdy one that had the least amount of moss and fungi, and pressed it into the ground to test if it would support me. When I found it satisfactory, I used it like a bridge to cross the clearing, and then continued on my way.

A tiny hill took me deeper into the woods, and there I was enclosed in color. Sunlight gleamed through the canopy like a prism, casting rays through the burning leaves, and when the wind rustled through the forest, it sent the leaves flying around me. I watched them dance to the ground, carpeting the path even thicker. *This truly is God's glory*, I thought. I wandered into the cluster of this creation, winding through twists and admiring how I felt like I was in a fairytale.

But I was so preoccupied with the beauty before me I hadn't noticed the path taking a sharper incline and narrowing to only a few feet in width. I came to a divide and realized I could see the street just down below, engines humming as cars raced by. The trees were less dressed than they'd been on the other side, some barely holding leaves to their branches. How quickly my beautiful woods had turned to a place I hardly recognized!

This is something we've also experienced in our spiritual journeys. We catch sight of something shiny and golden, and as we make our way toward it, the pleasure of admiring it distracts us from realizing until it's too late that we've wandered too deep into the woods. Suddenly, nothing looks familiar and we're not sure how to find our way back to the paths God wants us to take. Maybe the shiny thing is a pretty facade that camouflages something pernicious, something that will stimulate us for a while as it dulls and drains the spiritual nourishment and right desires of our hearts. Maybe the golden thing is something of genuine beauty, something God truly wants us to have, but we've become so invested in pursuing it that we've unwittingly taken a path that's led us away from the one who should be our ultimate pursuit. Either way, the result is lostness. How easy it is to walk deeper into the unknown and stray from God's love!

When we find ourselves off the path of God's goodness, how do we veer back? When the dazzle of this world distracts and distances us from the true life and light that Jesus offers, it's time to reorient ourselves and heed true beauty.

The Lord will guide you always.

ISAIAH 58:11

The Lord *will* guide us always. It's right there in his Word, a promise to us that he will show us the way. God does not withhold his path until we clean ourselves up enough to be deemed worthy of walking on it. His compassion is all-encompassing, and our hearts long for the true joy that comes through aligning with his path of righteousness. He longs to walk with us as we navigate this world, and he wants us to keep our attention on him instead of getting sidetracked by whatever sights and sounds the enemy teases us with. He wants us to listen to the truth he shares with us rather than the lies we hear from the world and even from ourselves. And when we turn our heads to better see what has enticed us, he takes our faces in his hands to gently redirect our gaze.

He guides me along the right paths for his name's sake.
PSALM 23:3

Look for the sun between the branches. Listen for the birdsong of God's lasting peace and grace rather than the tinny whirl of the world's easy and fleeting distractions. God's guidance is best for us, and it will lead us to the path of righteousness if we align our hearts to hear his voice through the noise that tries to throw us off course. True radiance is basking in the glow of God's glory, warming our hearts and following him further into right living for the sake of his kingdom and our good.

The Son is the radiance of God's glory and the exact representation of his being, sustaining all things by his powerful word. After he had provided purification for sins, he sat down at the right hand of the Majesty in heaven.
HEBREWS 1:3

We can step with certainty on the path he has prepared for us, for we know that his light is what truly shines.

REFLECT

What has taken your attention from God? Where can he meet your heart and bring you back on the path with him?

What would it look like for you to take confidence that he will guide you always?

LINGER

Psalm 25:9; Matthew 14:31; John 16:13

RESPOND

Oh Lord, I am so fickle in my faith. I stray from your love, your Word, and your grace to find pleasure in the things of this world that do not last. All that is gold will turn to rust, but you stay shining. Thank you that you still guide me and still lead me back to your beautiful arms. You are gracious, and merciful beyond all reason. Let me stay on your path. In Jesus' name, amen.

PRAISE

"Walk with You" by SEU Worship featuring Dan Rivera

24

THOSE WHO WAIT

Finding Refuge When We're Hurting

LONGINGS LIE OPEN. PSALM 38:9

May 2020

Eric's voice wakes me from a contented sleep. There is urgency in it, and I try to gauge where his voice is coming from as I shift myself awake. I find him in the bathroom, doubled over, unnaturally pale, drenched in sweat.

We had arrived on Washington Island, our favorite oasis, for our honeymoon, holed away in a hand-hewn log cabin rich with history, down the ridge at the edge of the shores of Lake Michigan. Here, we had begun our lives together, but now, at 2 a.m. with the last ferry to the mainland long gone, we are trapped, my husband of 36 hours heaving as broken breaths rack his giant body.

I call 911 in between pockets of reception, stroking Eric's back. An hour later, we are on an emergency ferry over the choppy night waters, headed to the mainland to transfer ambulances. Once we're there, we wind slowly through curving roads for an hour to the nearest hospital.

I am exhausted and alert in the waiting room while Eric is rolled into surgery for an appendix that's *this close* to rupturing. Prayer is my only solace.

When the panic presses in, we can shift into autopilot, our minds jumbled with one thought after another. Our questions unanswerable in the moment, we are helpless. The only thing we can do is turn to the one who has held us this far in our lives, as we endure a test of whether we believe he will still hold us through this.

All my longings lie open before you,
Lord; my sighing is not hidden from you.
PSALM 38:9

Our hearts are exposed when we're faced with crisis. There's no pretending we're put together; it's all we can do to not be undone. When results are unknown, when worry keeps us wound up through the night, we have nothing left but to rely on the faith we have, and we cry out to our Abba for mercy, strength, protection, and care.

All our longings and groans are laid out before him. Nothing is hidden. But in our hearts' desperate cry, here is where our Father meets us, reminds us of who he is, and that he is here. In the upside-down diagnosis, the experimental treatment, and the long nights pacing awake and weary, he is our good Father, our comforter, our companion. We are not alone in the darkness, for the dark is like light to him (Psalm 139:12).

When we are flat on the floor, worn down and desperate, his kindness reaches in and holds us. God doesn't promise to take away the pain in that moment, but he promises to be Immanuel, God *with* us, through the hurt, through the surprises and the overwhelm. We can run toward God when we are scared, because he truly is the only one who holds us together when we feel like falling apart.

Lord, I wait for you; you will answer, Lord my God.

PSALM 38:15

Eric made it out of surgery, and though I couldn't see him in post-op because of COVID regulations, I FaceTimed him in increments until he was released from the hospital. I cashed in my marriage vows right away, and amid this, I experienced God's vow to never leave or forsake me in comforting ways I needed to receive (Hebrews 13:5).

He will never leave nor forsake us. The Lord is good to those who wait and put their trust in him (Lamentations 3:25). Weeping may endure for a night, but joy comes in the morning (Psalm 30:5). We can trust him with the groans of our hearts; he hears and is right there with us, mighty to save, gentle to quiet us with his love (Zephaniah 3:17). Rest in the comfort that he cares and will see you through.

REFLECT

Remember a time of trial when you were in complete dependance on God to come through. What did that feel like?

Lay your longing out before the Lord today and ask him to comfort you in your pain.

LINGER

Psalm 38; Psalm 139:11-12; Matthew 28:20

RESPOND

Father, I didn't see this coming, but I believe you are with me. Here are my groans and longings, my questions and fears. Take them. Hold me. Be near to me and be my safe space and comfort. I have nothing to hold on to but you, and I am asking you to watch over my heart. You are my God, and you will never leave me. In Jesus' name, amen.

PRAISE

"Answers" by Caitie Hurst

25

MADE FOR THIS?

Cultivating Christlike Ambition

A QUIET LIFE. **1 THESSALONIANS 4:11**

In this world, there's always a higher height to reach. I can get trapped in the circus that is climbing the social ladder, pushing to pursue my purpose, longing to do and be as much as I can. I find myself pouring into my writing, my ministry, my work, and the people around me because that's what I'm supposed to do, right? Isn't this what God wants for me?

But that self-imposed pressure for perfection can swiftly send me into overdrive, spiking my stress levels once again. And what is it that I'm really seeking? A sustainable career? A gold star from God? There is so much to keep up with, and combining life's daily tasks with my personal pursuits of—dare I admit it?—glory and good marks opens the door for things to go sideways fast.

Even as Christians, we can succumb too easily to the worldly pressure to be all we can be, whatever we think that means for us. We can even mistake this striving for obedience to God. Striving comes from our own effort, fueled by dependency on what we do, whereas following our calling comes from the overflow of knowing we are already loved by God as we obediently take the steps he's laid out before us. It's not bad to have goals, whether those goals are earning a PhD, starting a family, running a half-marathon, or throwing ourselves into ministry.

But the striving and stress of holding these goals up high as our greatest prize will inevitably take away from our ability to see the God who has given us drive and good things in the first place.

Our days rush by, each filled to the brim. But we were not made to keep taking on more, our minds and calendars swelling and leaving us with no room to slow down, step back, and *be* with the Lord. Eventually, our own efforts at excellence will leave us lacking. We can try to have everything and do it all, but this isn't sustainable. We can nobly pursue what God has invited us into, like being a wife, mother, or ministry worker, but if we lesson our time with God and let ambition lead us instead, we lose our first love in the Lord and are found lacking. There is *more* for us in *less*.

The priority is making effort to stay close to the Lord. We may not be able to take everything off our plates, but we can prioritize seeking him in our quiet moments. Life with him is the aim of our days, wherever they take us.

Make it your ambition to lead a quiet life:
You should mind your own business and work with your
hands, just as we told you, so that your daily life may
win the respect of outsiders and so that you will not be
dependent on anybody.
1 THESSALONIANS 4:11-12

Note the type of ambition Paul suggests: the ambition to lead a quiet life, tucked in the folds of obscurity, settled in who God says we are and living comfortably in our lane. Our own modest ambitions are good—owning and maintaining a home, finding a job with good health insurance, exercising to keep our bodies healthy—but we mustn't let them overshadow our pursuit of God. Anything that comes in the way of prioritizing God first will leave us empty and lead us astray. We may have found ourselves caught in the trap of placing too much focus on the next thing—for more influential people in our lives, more purpose, a better body, or a bigger following. But this empty striving gets us nowhere but stuck on the wheel of discontent.

> "Meaningless! Meaningless!" says the Teacher.
> "Utterly meaningless! Everything is meaningless."
> **ECCLESIASTES 1:2**

What truly matters? Our good jobs, our beautiful homes, our physical strength will fade. Our relationships matter, and friends and family members will cherish the love we show them—however, while our love can have a lasting impact on their lives, we can serve them best not by pouring everything we have into our relationships with them, but by first filling ourselves with Christ's abundance and loving them out of his overflow. Why chase after the wind when the source of that wind is right in front of us, beckoning us closer to find contentment in him?

Paul has told us the secret to this contentment:

> I am not saying this because I am in need, for I have learned to be content whatever the circumstances. I know what it is to be in need, and I know what it is to have plenty. I have learned the secret of being content in any and every situation, whether well fed or hungry, whether living in plenty or in want. I can do all this through him who gives me strength (Philippians 4:11-13).

In all these things, Paul learned contentment in Christ. Lacking nothing and receiving everything, Paul set his heart on Jesus, who gave him strength and contentment.

We are precious to God just as we are, and he will see to all we need (Matthew 6:26). Let's set our eyes on God, the one who best knows what we need and who gives of himself freely, so we can nestle into his safe arms and let him calm the chaos spun by our chasing.

A quiet life caught up in Christ is a life worth living. That means taking the lesser road and appreciate the journey God has set before us rather than steaming past to reach the destination of the goals we've set for ourselves. As Paul says in Colossians 3:23, in everything we do, let us first think of God, aligning every heartbeat and action as an outpouring of praise to him.

It's exhausting to try to keep up with what we were never meant to have in the first place. Let it all go, the striving and the cramming of calendars. Our new lives are now hidden in Christ (Colossians 3:3), and what a beautiful place that is!

His kingdom matters; it's the one that will last. It is true and proper ambition to escape to a quiet place to recover our overworked souls (Mark 6:31).

Burnout does not become us. But a restful heart at home in God— now *that's* a life worth living.

REFLECT

What would that quiet life in the Lord look like to you?
How does your current daily schedule look in comparison?

Where do you find space for God in your current routine?

Are there areas in your life where you currently find yourself on the brink of burnout?

LINGER

Psalm 131; Proverbs 29:23; 1 John 3:2

RESPOND

Oh Lord, I've been caught up in striving and trying to create a life you are proud of. But it is burning me out and not healthy for my soul. I want to live a quiet life in you, but the pace of this world makes it hard to do. Would you show me what it looks like to get away with you and receive the rhythms of grace that you give? I am quieting my heart to hear from you. In Jesus' name, amen.

PRAISE

"Presence" by LO Worship

26

PRESENT-TENSE HOPE

Moving from Disappointment to Expectancy

WE HAD HOPED. **LUKE 24:21**

I had hoped…

It's a familiar phrase I've gotten used to repeating in this season of my life.

I had hoped my intrusive thoughts would disappear completely by now.

I had hoped my energy would be fully back to normal.

I had hoped my faith would not be threatened by panic attacks.

Can you relate? Perhaps for you it sounds more like:

I had hoped I'd get better from this long-lasting illness.

I had hoped I'd be married by now.

I had hoped this family conflict would resolve.

I had hoped.

We pray and search for a silver lining in the seemingly endless wait for what we want. It's disheartening, looking for the good things and outcomes we want to see, or perhaps watching others receive the blessings we've desired for ourselves—a partner, a house, a job.

Placing our hope in our situations improving leaves us exhausted and takes our eyes off the promises of God. We begin to feel doubt, even when we still ardently believe in and love God, even when we *know* he has our lives in his control. But it's hard to hold on when the long-awaited answers to our prayers don't seem to be coming. When doubt digs in, hope may seem abstract and far away. We know God keeps his promises of heaven, but in this life, we wonder if the promises we cling to will come to pass.

I know of some disciples of Jesus who understood this too. Days after Jesus' crucifixion, two disciples walked the road from Jerusalem to a town called Emmaus, their sandaled feet kicking up dust, their broken hearts heavy with disappointment (Luke 24:13). They were mourning the man they *had hoped* was the promised Messiah. They talked to each other in disbelief about the latest news they'd heard: Some women had gone to his tomb but hadn't found his body.

When the resurrected Jesus joined them, they did not recognize him! He listened to them recall the last few days' happenings, and then he unfolded the Scriptures and prophesies that described the Messiah, but still they could not see him for who he was.

What confounded them so? What held their hearts back from understanding?

Initially, they couldn't recognize Jesus because their hope was in the past tense. They "*had hoped* that he was the one who was going to redeem Israel" (Luke 24:21, emphasis added). They had a specific idea of what it would look like for Israel to be redeemed, so when Jesus was crucified, they assumed it was a lost cause. They'd given up their hope that Jesus was the Savior Israel awaited, even as Jesus miraculously stood before them, confronting them with the Scriptures that made clear that he *was* Israel's Messiah.

When the risen Jesus revealed himself by taking the time to walk with them to Emmaus and engaging with them through conversation and breaking bread, the men were amazed. Revived hope fanned their faith back into flame: "They said to each other, 'Did not our hearts burn within us while he talked to us on the road, while he opened to us the Scriptures?'" (Luke 24:32 ESV).

Jesus showed he *is* the one who redeems, even though he didn't do it the way everyone thought he would. And thankfully, when Jesus adjusts our eyes and hearts to see the purpose he brings and who he really is, our understanding of what it means to place our hope in him changes.

May the God of hope fill you with all joy and peace as you trust in him, so that you may overflow with hope by the power of the Holy Spirit.

ROMANS 15:13

Have you started thinking about certain hopes in the past tense? Do you have prayers you've stopped praying because you no longer believe God will answer them? What will it take to change your heart to hinge on Jesus, the resurrected one who came through for us just as he said he would?

What might we be missing, even as we walk with Jesus, if we don't remind ourselves that he's the Savior who does the impossible, who listens to us and takes time to share his heart with us? What might be holding us back from understanding the hope he offers us, not just for eternity but for right now?

We can get honest with God. We can unpack the burdens that have been holding us back, and we can listen to what he says based on his Word and character. Let him know the things you've hoped for, and know that it's okay to share if your heart is heavy because they haven't come to pass. When we give ourselves space to sift through the disappointment of unfulfilled dreams, we give ourselves room to reflect more deeply on our faith, and time to notice any faults or fractures. Might there be somewhere God wants to help us refocus our trust away from a desired outcome and replace it with deeper trust in him?

Reflect on the character of Jesus and reflect on where you've placed your hope. Cling to the present-tense hope we have in him, because he gives us what we need, in his time (Philippians 4:19).

When Jesus came, he gave us an eternal perspective. His life, death, and resurrection demonstrate that we cannot see all the ways God is at work—but even this mystery invites us into deeper intimacy with him. Jesus will handle what we cannot see in the ways he knows are best for us. In the meantime, we need to adjust our preconceived timelines and reconsider our ideas of how it will look for our dreams to be fulfilled. We can still trust and wait for God to come through for us, but part of how he may do that is by loosening our expectations and stirring us to surrender to his timing and ways. He is faithful. We can trust that he is at work providing for us today.

Let's shift our perspective to present-tense hope in our Savior. We can be certain his heart toward us *is* good. He is the giver of good gifts (James 1:17), and his presence is the greatest gift of all. His heart toward us is full of hope, life, and joy. Let's strengthen our hearts as we wait in expectancy for him to come through, however that ends up looking. Because our living God *will* come through; he has already shown himself faithful. We can trust he is making a way.

REFLECT

Have you put your hope in a dream that hasn't happened yet? How can you lean into the promises of Jesus to take you into a deeper and lasting hope in him?

To take a different look at an unfulfilled need or desire that has caused you anguish, invite God into it, and refocus your hope in God working for your good and his glory. Share with him the pain, grief, and fear you have experienced because of this burden, but also remind yourself that your hope in God is greater even than this circumstance.

LINGER

Luke 24:5-7; Romans 6:4; 1 Peter 1:3

RESPOND

Father, I am weary from wanting. I've been dreaming and hoping for a long time, and what I desire hasn't come to pass. I don't understand why I've had this prayer in my heart for so long only for it to go unanswered. I am discouraged, and I don't know how much longer I should hope for this. But you are my comfort; I can look at your love and remember that you care about my heart. What you have in store for me is good, and you are providing for me even now. Thank you that you are faithful in my life. I wait on you. In Jesus' name, amen.

PRAISE

"A Hope and a Future" by Fresh Life Worship

BROKEN BRANCHES:

RELATIONAL STRAIN

It should be straightforward: right through the woods. But the paths are overgrown and scattered with sticks and brush. Thick logs from fallen trees block the way, and we have to hoist ourselves over the hurdles. Twigs twist and crack beneath our feet, the hands of branches swiping our faces as we walk. It's hard to see through the canopy, resetting our footing from an overgrown root jutting from the earthen floor. The forest looks as scattered as we feel. Dusk approaches, shadows grow, and haphazard trees groan beneath their broken-off limbs.

We desire relationships with others, whether that's with friends, family, a spouse, or our community. It's placed in us, a deep and insatiable desire to be seen, known, and accepted. Which is why it's unbearable when those ties sever, when the sharp blade of disconnect slices through to pierce our hearts. It wrecks us. Strain and separation were never meant to be part of our everyday lives. God created us to reflect union, and we are meant to fuse together, not break apart.

It stings, the cut of loneliness, the relational strain that separates friends and family. That can lead us down a slippery slope of comparing how our lives have turned out to those we think have it all together. What can help us get through when relationships near and dear to us dissolve or we're a little *too* familiar with being alone?

27

SOMEONE TO LEAN ON

Letting the Lord Ease Our Loneliness

BY HIS WOUNDS. **1 PETER 2:24**

Loneliness is an ache that lingers. When our dearly beloved betrays us, when sharp words from a close friend cut too deep, when the hope for a whole and healed family continues to unravel, we often find ourselves tucked away at the end of the day examining the wounds of our hearts. What went wrong? Was it something we did? What could we have done or said to make things better? The list of what-ifs goes on and on in our heads, while our hearts still throb.

Being alone hurts. Will this loneliness ever go away? What do we do with the desires of our hearts that don't seem to come to fruition?

Yet this unrelenting sadness will not swallow us down. God will not allow it. We may not see a way out, but *we* are seen, we are known, and we are cherished.

God knows every ache and crevice where our pain is stored, and he tracks our tears (Psalm 56:8). His heart hurts with ours, and he wants us to know that he enters those empty places with the longing to fill them. He longs for us to experience him more intimately, to know him in a deeper way, to be the one who comforts us, holds us, and slowly replaces the ache of isolation with a love that fills us.

Jesus knows affliction, abandonment, and betrayal. He came to this world knowing that it would be hard, and recognizing that there would be strained relationships, times when he felt alone, periods when his own spirit was crushed in agony. But he endured it all, for us. Because he knew what it felt like to be pounded down by pain, he could meet us in ours, tend to our wounds, and assure us that we will never truly be alone.

He himself bore our sins in his body on the tree,
that we might die to sin and live to righteousness.
By his wounds you have been healed.

1 PETER 2:24 ESV

It's amazing, really. That the Lord of all creation would come near us. That he wants us to lean into him, allow him a privileged place in our hearts. When you're in your bed depleted, tears pooling on your pillow, remember him, because he remembers you. He is aware of how you hurt, and he came to be broken so we no longer have to break down on our own. When we lean into him with our broken hearts, we experience the beginning of him transforming our forgottenness into belonging.

In him we belong, and in him we have found what we are made for (Acts 17:28). Will this finally satisfy our searching hearts? Is he enough for us? If we have nothing but him, can we close our eyes at night and say we are safe because we are in him? Scripture assures us that we can (Psalm 4:8). Jesus holds us while we hurt. By his wounds, our own wounds are healed—now and forever, we take comfort knowing that one day, when we are with him in heaven, all our tears will dry and all our pain will disappear. In *this* we can take comfort. Whether the wounds are fresh or festering, the salve is still the same: the love of Jesus.

The way he took on hurt in a whole new way for us to be comforted. The one who knew no sin bore our sin so we could be stainless before God (2 Corinthians 5:21). We'll never fully understand the impact of what he endured this side of heaven, but we can let him reassure our hearts that there is no situation where he can't bring us comfort.

Take heart. The ache may still be there, but you are certainly not alone in it. Jesus is your Sustainer, Comforter, and Healer. His love runs deep, connecting to our tattered hearts and drawing us to the heart and hope of God our Father. He has promised a love that never leaves. Let him be this to you in your sorrow, in your pain. His love is tender, and his heart is yours.

REFLECT

What has made your heart hurt today?

How can you let the God of comfort into your loneliness? When you feel like you're on your own, what stops you from remembering or accepting that he is with you?

LINGER

Psalm 25:16; Proverbs 18:24; Hebrews 4:15-16

RESPOND

Father, my heart hurts. The pain I'm feeling from this broken situation is breaking me. Would you come into this with me? Remind me of how I am not alone in my pain and sorrow, and that you long to come close to me in this. Jesus endured pain, too. He reminds me I am not alone. Help me rest in your comfort and love. In Jesus' name, amen.

PRAISE

"Father (Unplugged)" by Emilie Weiss

28

CARRIED CLOSER THROUGH CONFLICT

Receiving and Extending Compassion

CAST YOUR CARES. **PSALM 55:22**

It's a quick interaction and happens so fast I'm blindsided by the backlash. Getting caught in a barrage of words with a family member has made me defensive and disappointed, and it's only a matter of moments before I dissolve into tears. How could such an innocuous interaction turn so sour in a matter of seconds?

Wounds delivered by those closest to us cut the deepest. We care about what our family members, our spouses, our friends, our close colleagues think of us—we want to please them and find acceptance, and we want to keep the peace. What they say matters and means a lot, and when their words are harsh or critical, our tender hearts tend to fold into themselves in self-defense as our inner child cries from the hurt.

Close relationships matter, and something as simple as a stray word or misconstrued statement can spiral us into confusion, disappointment, and a temptation to take cruel words to heart. This surprising conversation with someone dear to me draws out the reality of what can happen when we're so fixed on our own perspective that we can't step outside it to see those around us.

Even if I never get an apology for the pain a loved one's thoughtless reaction has caused me, I must do the work of my heart and take my hurt to God.

Cast your cares on the LORD and he will sustain you;
he will never let the righteous be shaken.

PSALM 55:22

When we cast our cares on God, we toss them as far from ourselves as we can and let them fly, releasing the burden from our own shoulders and handing them to the one who can take them on while tending to the residual effects of the memories of hurt and frustration that have held us down. We exchange our heartbreak, our anger, our disappointment—whatever we are feeling—for God's calming presence and strength. He is for us (Romans 8:31) and wants to hold what we were never meant to hold onto: pain, bitterness, resentment, fear.

As we hand our hurt over, we are carried closer to the compassionate heart of God. God can do wonders with the people and circumstances that have brought us pain, and his desire is to bring us into closer relationship with him. If you're hurting, or in a place of confusion about how to handle a difficult relationship, let God in on your questions and uncertainty. No one knows the situation better than him, and in his great wisdom and love, God will guide you through the discomfort. He may not promise immediate relief or that everything will turn out the way we hope, but he does promise to sustain us as we stride ahead in our healing.

Jesus invites us to receive his lasting peace, because he knows this is what will resonate deep within us and transform our future interactions, even with that person who spoke a harsh word or doesn't seem to empathize with you.

Peace I leave with you; my peace I give you. I do not give to you as the world gives. Do not let your hearts be troubled and do not be afraid.

JOHN 14:27

Don't you long for this peace that goes beyond the world and curls into your heart? What would that look like lived in light of knowing that the God of the universe cares for your troubles and accepting Jesus' offer of deep and abiding peace?

If our hearts are in the right place with God, our hearts can be in the right place with others. Take the hurt and hurl it off your heart so it lands at the feet of our good and gracious God. It's his to handle. Now your job is to trust that he is doing a healing work in you, allowing you to turn your own compassion toward the one who has hurt you. God knows that person needs a little grace to get through this life, as we all do. And that's exactly what God longs to give to help our hearts unburden and no longer carry the weight of this trouble.

REFLECT

Have you been hurt by someone close to you? How did that make you feel? How has this pain affected your relationship with that person and with others?

How can you give your hurt and cares to the Lord today? What would that look like?

LINGER

Matthew 5:9; Romans 12:19; 1 Peter 5:7

RESPOND

Father, I'm reeling a bit from the backlash of what someone close to me has said. It hurt me, and I feel disappointed and like I let them down. Help me focus my attention on you and what you say about the conversation. Be my comfort and give me your peace that is better than anything I can try to produce on my own. In Jesus' name, amen.

PRAISE

"King of My Heart" by John Mark McMillan

29

NEVER ALONE

Loving God When Our Hearts Hurt for Romance

LILY OF THE VALLEYS. **SONG OF SONGS 2:1**

I was three weeks shy of my 35th birthday when I got married, and I didn't date much before I met Eric, so I spent a lot of time in singleness. I like to think that I was single-mindedly focused on Jesus, but waves of loneliness would stretch out time through the evenings when I became very aware that it was just me, myself, and I.

When I faced the temptation to think there might be something wrong with me to still be so incredibly single, I reminded myself of who I was in Christ. I trusted that he had the plans for my life perfectly in his hands, and that if it was indeed his plan to someday bring a man after his own heart into my life, it would be at the right time.

Still, it isn't easy to watch the years go by and see your relationship status stuck on single. And even if you're married, you might still relate to this loneliness if you feel alone even though you're sleeping next to the one to whom you've committed your life.

It isn't easy when:

You've read book after book, devouring chapters filled with heart-stirring romance and blazing gazes and whispered promises, but as the last page turns, four walls return and you're left alone and silent in the emptiness.

You've tried the warm arms of a cold heart, only to lay awake in the morning sifting through the ashes of a fire flamed out.

You've stood in the deli section of the grocery store, ticket in hand for shaved ham, noting how similar you feel to the piece of meat being weighed on the scale.

You've assessed yourself with practiced eyes in front of the mirror, magnifying every blemish, every wrinkle, every added curve until, like Dorian Gray's portrait, the reflection turns into a hideous monster.

You've watched friend after friend float down a petal-strewn aisle, your own bridesmaid dress fitting a bit too snug, pondering when it will be you tossing the bouquet instead of competing to catch it.

You've trailed rivers of tears down your pillow in the dark, replaying the events of hours earlier and asking yourself over and over why you just weren't enough.

It's a vulnerable place, that hidden hope in our hearts to share all of ourselves with another, so we hesitate to open up, skeptical anyone will truly see us and sweep us off our feet.

But look at who arrives to prove a love genuine and secure, who takes you in his arms and tells you he's seen you everywhere you've been: sitting in the corner of a coffee shop, sipping your favorite latte; jogging through a park, feet flying over the pavement, dreaming of what is to come; readying the second load of laundry, separating colors from whites.

Let the king be enthralled by your beauty;
honor him, for he is your lord.

PSALM 45:11

God wants to hold you in his arms and assure you that he is captivated by you. He sent his Son to save you. He is pleased with your presence and calls you beautiful (Song of Songs 2:10). He's intimately acquainted with you; he formed you purposefully and with intention (Psalm 139:13-14). He promises to never leave you or forsake you (Deuteronomy 31:6).

Christ's hands stained with scars hold your own, hold you in your desire to be seen and wanted. God replaces the repugnance we feel toward our aloneness with the warmth of his love, which fills our longing hearts and turns us to see a new reflection in the mirror: that of one who is beloved and cherished.

I am a rose of Sharon, a lily of the valleys.
SONG OF SONGS 2:1

Our situations may vary, but the core of them is the same: We are looking for someone to see us—really see us—in the depths and not walk away. To come close, to keep eye contact, and to tell us we are loved. The God who sees all we think, do, and say steps toward us and loves us with an all-encompassing love that transforms our hearts. We see ourselves in the eyes of Christ, and when the truth of his love settles in, we can remind ourselves of just how seen and valuable we are. We can say with certainty: "I am a rose of Sharon, a lily of the valleys" (Song of Songs 2:1).

The next time you're tempted to question whether you are seen and cared for, remind yourself that through God's deep love, you are never alone.

How have you handled your seasons of loneliness? What did you perceive about God?

Will you allow yourself to be loved by Jesus? What would this look like?

LINGER

Psalm 139; Zephaniah 3:17; Romans 5:8

RESPOND

Father, thank you for loving me, all of me—imperfections and all. May I fall more and more in love with you as I allow you to love me and remind me that I am never alone. May I seek after your heart and all you encourage me to be. In Jesus' name, amen.

PRAISE

"How Much More" by Rita Springer

30

EVERYTHING TO EVERYONE

Releasing the Burdens of Others

THE LORD GIVES STRENGTH. **PSALM 29:11**

I'm wiped. It's been months of a demanding travel schedule, long hours on a job I love, time with family visiting from out of state, and many writing deadlines. Add to that the pressure to keep up my social schedule with friends, Bible study, and a few other family obligations. I feel like I can't take much more on my plate, but demands continue to pile up.

Are you overloaded too? Have you taken on too much and given in to just a few too many "yeses" to your days or weeks? If time and attention for others have taken away our quiet with God, we can begin from empty before we even get started.

And what about the people whose needs extend beyond your capacity? Maybe they are asking for more time than you are able to give, or need emotional assurance that you just simply cannot afford? If you're already worn thin from meeting the needs of others, rest assured that you are not alone. The needs of others don't have to keep you from the abundant life Jesus holds out to you.

We don't have to keep the peace on our own. That is not a burden we need to bear. If someone is taking up more of your mental and emotional capacity than you are able to give at this time, recognize it. Yes, we are meant to share in one another's burdens, but first take assessment of your own life. Is your relationship with God first and foremost? Are you getting enough time with him on your own, or is something hindering you from staying connected to the source of your spiritual sustenance?

After that, ask yourself, who are the people in your close inner circle? How are your relationships there? If those are lacking, step back and assess why. After our relationship to God, our relationships to our spouse, our children, and immediate family are of next importance and concentration. Prioritize making sure those are healthy as they can be, and if God is leading you to take up more connection with someone, know that he will also equip you for the challenge (2 Corinthians 9:8).

Take your cares to God before anything else. Let him know how you feel about this situation or a particular person who is weighing heavy on your heart and mind.

The LORD gives strength to his people;
the LORD blesses his people with peace.

PSALM 29:11

He will give you strength, and he will also send you on the path to best dealing with this difficult person. Whether that's to step back with some well-earned boundaries or to limit yourself on how often you can listen to them share their burdens, God will let you know. We long for his peace, even while we shuffle between carrying the burdens of others and admitting our own shortcomings.

God knows how helpless you feel. He loves your loved one more than you do. He isn't unaware of the struggles, the desperation, the tears shed with your face in your hands at the letdown of it all. He holds you close, consoles you, and invites you to hand this over to him. Curl closer into his heart and receive his gentle and endless love. From that deep, soothing, strengthening love, his Spirit fills us while strengthening us to step back into the relationships he has called us into.

Above all, love each other deeply,
because love covers over a multitude of sins.

1 PETER 4:8

When you find yourself on the receiving end of someone's problem and emotional need, keep directing that person to God. We can't carry their loads, but we can lead them to the one who can.

Let God's peace lead you and bless you. He is always enough for whatever overload you're facing, always sustaining and strengthening your inner being to be a blessing of peace to those in desperate need of the God who is always enough for all of us.

REFLECT

What relationships are weighing you down? How have you handled them in the past?

How can you invite God into your exhaustion so he can fill you with strength and grace?

LINGER

Philippians 2:3; Colossians 3:12; 1 Thessalonians 5:15

RESPOND

Lord, I admit I'm overloaded. My life is far too full, and I don't have the emotional capacity to love the people around me like I should. Fill me with your grace, which is greater than anything else I could need. Soften my heart to love like you, and when I am invited into someone's burden, may I bring them to you. In Jesus' name, amen.

PRAISE

"Hands of the Healer" by Hope Darst

31

FORGIVENESS FINDS THE LIGHT

Turning Toward Repentance

LOVE IS PATIENT. **1 CORINTHIANS 13:4**

February 2021

Eric walks through the door with a bouquet of flowers on a random Thursday. But something sets me off, and even though I know I'm overreacting to such a kind gesture, I can't stop myself from railing against the blue and white hydrangeas, protesting I don't need them, and distancing myself from my husband of eight months. All this over flowers, directed toward someone and something I've dreamed of for years—a caring husband who for no reason wants to gift me with beauty.

But I am not one for surprises, and the last few years of my life have been nothing but. A stroke and heart procedure, multiple moves, meeting and marrying Eric in the span of one short year, and all these months of adjustment to life spent with another person in the middle of a global pandemic—yes, life has pushed my tolerance for change to the edge. I like time to process, think, and feel, room to lean in with God so I can unearth his subtle lessons.

But we notice our growth in patterns of growing pains. It takes me about half an hour to take space, calm down, and understand my reaction. Once I've remembered that Eric is a safe place, I am ashamed by the hurt I've inflicted in response to his gesture of love, and the precious time I've wasted going off at him. When I go to apologize, my eyes find his, and I know I am immediately forgiven when I see his love still clearly reflected in those calm pools of blue. He isn't going anywhere, and I don't want him to. His arms stretch wide to welcome me back into his embrace, and without a word, I understand forgiveness and grace with new depth. Those words take on greater meaning when put into action, and through Eric's simple, "I love you," I am drawn closer to Jesus.

Love is patient, love is kind. It does not envy, it does not boast, it is not proud. It does not dishonor others, it is not self-seeking, it is not easily angered, it keeps no record of wrongs. Love does not delight in evil but rejoices with the truth. It always protects, always trusts, always hopes, always perseveres.

1 CORINTHIANS 13:4-7

Marriage reminds me that I'm more selfish and headstrong than I thought. Too often, I am confronted with the chance to break my pride and ask forgiveness after I have hurt my husband. It's hard to fight against the part of me that wants to stay angry and prideful, but through all circumstances, I am called to seek peace and unity with Eric, whom God has given to me. And I ask God to remind me to seek Eric's good, to step out into the vast waters of empathy and repentance after I've slung a slicing word his way or created distance between us. Many times, I fail drastically, yet every time, Eric offers me that safe place to return.

Relationships are refining. God uses them to mirror how he sees and loves us.

Love is patient. When we get stuck on tangential rants, God listens until we are finished, then reaches us with a soft voice that redirects our minds while comforting our hearts.

Be completely humble and gentle; be patient,
bearing with one another in love.
EPHESIANS 4:2

Love is kind. God doesn't engage in name-calling or unfair fights. He looks past our emotion-driven responses, sees the wounds that afflict us, and addresses where we've acted out of anger or refused to ask forgiveness because of pride. He understands why we've lashed out even better than we do, because he already understands perfectly that we have been fractured by the world; he already knows that people who have been hurt inevitably hurt other people. This doesn't mean that God writes off our wrongdoing as inconsequential, but that he meets our brokenness with his incredible compassion and mercy.

Dear children, let us not love with words or speech but
with actions and in truth.
1 JOHN 3:18

Love does not envy or boast, nor is it proud. Jesus keeps us humble and helps us to avoid the self-prioritization we tend to cling to in conflict. He protects our relationship with him, holds a mirror to our hearts, and gently asks us what our deeper issue is. Then, Jesus generously gives us the chance to recognize the errors of our way, to repent of how we've hurt him and the ones we have wronged, and to seek true forgiveness and restoration.

If my people, who are called by my name, will humble themselves and pray and seek my face and turn from their wicked ways, then I will hear from heaven, and I will forgive their sin and will heal their land.

2 CHRONICLES 7:14

On and on it goes, grace and love from the overflow of Jesus. Never would we have imagined that we'd experience *more* of God in the wake of our shame and humiliation, when we recognize we've acted wrongly and hurt the ones we love the most. Jesus said to forgive seventy times seven (Matthew 18:21-22), and our loved ones have graciously utilized a good portion of that equation on us.

Let's let our own actions toward others match the ways of Jesus. Do we allow Jesus' work in us to love those around us more than ourselves? Do we strive to keep the chords of unity in perfect harmony? Do we vulnerably allow Jesus and our close loved ones into the places we'd rather keep hidden?

As God's chosen people, holy and dearly loved, clothe yourselves with compassion, kindness, humility, gentleness and patience. Bear with each other and forgive one another if any of you has a grievance against someone. Forgive as the Lord forgave you. And over all these virtues put on love, which binds them all together in perfect unity (Colossians 3:12-14).

Remember forgiveness and love meet together in the same breath. Love is patient and kind, bears no wrongs. What a beautiful freedom we find when forgiveness finds the light and our hearts are exposed and healed. This repentance and restoration lead us to better love God, and better love those with whom he has placed us in relationships.

REFLECT

Is there someone you need to forgive? Is there someone whose forgiveness you need to ask? What does it look like to take those next steps?

How does knowing that you have God's unconditional forgiveness affect the way you interact with him and others?

LINGER

Mark 11:25; Luke 6:37; Ephesians 1:7

RESPOND

Love is patient, love is kind. Thank you, God, that you show me the best example of love in the way you have forgiven me. Thank you that your mercies are new every morning, and you are eager to cover me through the blood of Christ. Help me extend mercy and forgiveness to others, and live out of the overflowing grace you have given me. In Jesus' name, amen.

PRAISE

"What He's Done" by Passion

32

LEAN IN, LET GO

Healing from Relationship Hurt

CLOSER THAN A BROTHER. **PROVERBS 18:24**

We were like sisters. We shared in each other's lives, played on all the same sports teams, and were at each other's houses like we both lived in two places. My best friend and I were inseparable, and my loyal heart attached early in middle school and fiercely guarded and defended our friendship. But when we began to drift my junior year in high school, my heart unraveled as she spent more time with other crowds and the calls to hang out came less and less. I tried to play it off like it didn't bother me, but it broke my young heart. I treasured our friendship, and the slow dissolution of our relationship while still playing on the same basketball team tore me up. As a teenager, I fretted over unanswered questions: What had happened? Had I done something wrong? Was I not enough for her?

Decades later, I still remember this pain. Whether we play it off or let ourselves feel the hurt, lost friendships sting. The heart attachments we make fuse our affections to another, and when those forged bonds break, those cuts can run deep. Maybe you too have a broken bond that has left you wondering what went wrong, and whether the answer points to you. Maybe you're still deflecting the harsh words slung in your direction or having to see smiling faces via social media that remind you of one more gathering you weren't invited to.

What can help us get through when relationships near and dear to us dissolve? Placing our loneliness with the one who knows the shadows of alone.

He was despised and rejected by mankind,
a man of suffering, and familiar with pain.
Like one from whom people hide their faces he was
despised, and we held him in low esteem.

ISAIAH 53:3

We're in good company when the one familiar with pain and from whom people hid their face turns to you in comfort and knowing. Jesus can tenderly empathize with our feelings of rejection and despair.

He was rejected by men, abandoned by his friends, and left alone on the cross, where he cried out to his Father and received silence as response.

About three in the afternoon Jesus cried out in a
loud voice, "Eli, Eli, lema sabachthani?"
(which means "My God, my God,
why have you forsaken me?").

MATTHEW 27:46

Scourged, exhausted both physically and spiritually, and set up to suffer under a very public viewing of a sinner's death, Jesus had no one at the end of his life. He went through all he did to save and redeem the world. But he also endured suffering and abandonment so intense that he sweated drops of blood in anguish (Luke 22:44). He could empathize with everything we go through as humans.

Thank God that *we* are never alone! Jesus endured the cross and that unbearable aloneness so those who believe in him would never have to endure this ultimate loneliness. He is our Redeemer and Restorer. He is the one who protectively scoops us in his arms and holds us while we cry, listens while we talk about being abandoned and alone.

Friends come and go, but Christ Jesus will always be with us.

One who has unreliable friends soon comes to ruin,
but there is a friend who sticks closer than a brother.

PROVERBS 18:24

He is loyal. He is faithful. He sees your hurt and the tears from lost friendships. You are seen, your hurts are recognized and validated, and you have a loving Lord who walks with you. Christ stays the same yesterday, today, and forever (Hebrews 13:8), and his presence is one we can truly rely on. In him we can find a lasting relationship that fills us with hope, healing, beauty, and trust. Lean into the love he offers. Let go of the lost time and memories, and draw closer to the Lord. Hold him close in those weary places; he is already holding you.

REFLECT

How have you handled people coming and going in your life? Do you have any wounds left by broken relationships that still need to be healed? Invite God to begin this healing process in you.

How does knowing Jesus experienced loneliness help you navigate yours?

LINGER

Psalm 38:9; Matthew 28:20; John 14:18

RESPOND

Lord, sometimes the loneliness gets to be too much. Sometimes I feel like I am always looking for someone to see me as I am and still genuinely love me. Lord, you are that person. Thank you for sending your Son to endure the cross and experience a lonely life. Help me remember that Jesus made a way for me. Be with me in my loneliness. Thank you for staying with me. In Jesus' name, amen.

PRAISE

"Let Not Your Heart Be Troubled" by Jillian Edwards

33

GRACE IS GREATER

Watching Our Words

A GENTLE ANSWER. **PROVERBS 15:1**

I can be mean.

I can sling reckless words at my tender-hearted husband and slice him where he is most prone to bleeding. Without blinking, I can spew out statements that cause harm. My words can come fast and furious, hardly able to keep up with my dark heart. Like thunderclouds rolling in, the storm of fury arrives swiftly and on target.

Once I've gotten everything out of my system, I may feel remorse, but the damage is done. I can't take back what I've hurled in my self-absorbed storm, can't erase the truth that I've hurt the one who means the most to me.

A gentle answer turns away wrath, but a harsh word stirs up anger. The tongue of the wise adorns knowledge, but the mouth of the fool gushes folly. The eyes of the Lord *are everywhere, keeping watch on the wicked and the good. The soothing tongue is a tree of life, but a perverse tongue crushes the spirit.*

PROVERBS 15:1-4

Our human tendencies pull us toward sending a tongue lashing to those around us, especially the ones we feel most comfortable with. Yet this does nothing but destroy and tear down. Does it make us feel good to get it out? Do we realize what damage we've just done? Do we even consider how it makes the person on the receiving end feel?

Words have power.

Words are tools that can turn into weapons.

Words can wound.

A small spark of speech can set off a firestorm of destruction (James 3:5-6). Do we want to be gentle with our words, or do we want to be harsh and cause hurt?

Resentment grows when we don't address the deeper issues that are causing buildup and blockage in us. The more we push down feelings of sadness, anger, resentment, and disappointment, the more prone they are to emerge unexpectedly in loose speech when that anger boils to the surface.

From the unhappiness in our hearts flows the way our words go.

The tongue has the power of life and death,
and those who love it will eat its fruit.

PROVERBS 18:21

God knows our hearts are deceitful (Jeremiah 17:9) and understands that we can not only hurt others with our outbursts, but ourselves. What corrodes us from the inside when we don't deal with what's irritating us can turn into a long-term problem. And God has healing and hope for us; he doesn't want us weighed down by destructive thoughts and feelings (Philippians 4:8).

Words can also be wielded for good, to bring a salve to what has stung us. When we speak words of life, healing and connection happen. Our inner turmoil subsides, and we are brought closer to the heart of God to get at the heart of the matter. When we come with words of grace and gentleness, we allow others to open up more easily about what has hurt them, and there we can share the truth and grace of God.

Words can be a refuge, somewhere we find shelter in the warmth of assurance and hope. Words can be a fortress, giving us strength to stand firm in who we've been called to be, step into the character someone has called out in us and live into it. We hold the power of life and death in the blessings we speak or the curses we call down.

A gentle answer turns away wrath,
but a harsh word stirs up anger.

PROVERBS 15:1

Before we verbally batter our best friend or husband or child, or even the clerk checking us out at the grocery store, let's check our hearts and ask what is making us feel angry or unheard. Sifting through the rubble of our feelings, we can unearth the root of our problem and give an honest assessment before God. He isn't afraid of what we find, and he has ways of fixing it once and for all.

It's hard to restrain our speech in the heat of the moment, but it's holy work to let the Lord teach our tongue to hold back words that tear down and replace them instead with words that strengthen.

As Christians, our goal cannot be to knock our loved ones down a peg with the propulsion of unkind speech. It must be the opposite:

We should want to see them as beloved in Christ and made in God's image. What we say to them, we say to God.

Gracious words are a honeycomb,
sweet to the soul and healing to the bones.
PROVERBS 16:24

I have no excuse for the ways I've let my words stray and slap at Eric's heart. These words are unkind and untruthful. And they certainly do not build him up. But thank God, he shows me forgiveness when I ask, an example to me of the forgiveness God also shows.

It's sweeter to let the good stuff pour from our speech, and much gentler on our hearts when we visibly see the good our words can do when delivered with love.

God's intention for each of us to have toward each other is unity, and that is woven when our words are used to care for, comfort, and encourage. We can make it our ambition to shift the way we speak. If we slip up, we can seek forgiveness, then start again. God will equip you to do this hard but holy work because his desire is to change your heart where it has been misguided.

We can change the tone of our voice. From the overflow of grace, we can be a source of hope and help when we use our words to speak the love and truth of Christ.

REFLECT

When have you been quick to speak without considering the consequences? What has been the impact of these unwisely chosen words?

How can you start inviting God into your thoughts and words today? When it comes to what you say and how you speak, do you have any bad habits you need to begin breaking?

LINGER

Proverbs 4:20-22; Proverbs 16:23; Ephesians 4:29

RESPOND

Father, I can be so careless with my tongue. I am quick to talk, to always have the last word, to be sharp with those I love. Help me curb my tongue, to check my heart and pay attention to what is making me unhappy. Replace my bitterness with your joy and peace, and may my words build up more than tear down. In Jesus' name, amen.

PRAISE

"Here's My Heart" by Lauren Daigle

34

A LITTLE EXTRA GENTLENESS

Handling Hard People

BE KIND AND COMPASSIONATE. **EPHESIANS 4:32**

We all know them: the kind of people who can't seem to give us any grace. No matter what we say or how we say it, our sentiments are not received as desired. It can be maddening, trying to engage with someone who won't see the in-between or meet us in the middle. We waver back and forth between empathizing with their pain and building a buffer between us and them to keep our peace of mind and spirit.

We want to love like Jesus, but we have human emotions we can't ignore either. How do we operate with a Christlike heart while handling disagreements or the unyielding demands of others?

We prepare to give a little extra gentleness and grace, listening while keeping our own hearts healthy in the process. We look to the Lord to lead us in these conversations because we ourselves have been on the receiving end of God's gentleness, and the grace he has poured out to us through Christ we can then share from our heart's overflow. We trust God to give us greater compassion, to fill us with his love, and then turn that love toward those with whom we have a disagreement, seeing them through the eyes of Jesus, knowing they need the same love of God that we have received.

We can't control what people say or how they respond. And we have a right to stand on God's truth and set boundaries when we need to protect ourselves and our families. But we *can* respond and relate to others with kindness, compassion, and grace.

What looks like Jesus? What is God after in these strained relationships that seem to rile us up and take an emotional toll? He calls us to look deeper into our hearts, asking us to let him see those places where we still need the nourishment of knowing the width, length, height, and depth of the love of Christ. He lets that love permeate our being, and brings us into deeper intimacy with the Father (Ephesians 3:18-19).

From the fullness of God, we are filled, readied for a fruitful existence with him and each other. When we are immersed in God's love, we grow in his grace and knowledge (2 Peter 3:18) as it becomes a habit to have that grace always before us and direct us in what we say, *how* we say it, and how we interact.

God is always calling us to become more like him. And unsettling conversations with people from whom we desire peace bring us opportunities to see what is under the surface of our actions and assess the posture of our hearts. Here we are invited to experience God not just in word but deed.

Our own tempers can flare when we feel offended. Our frustrations flourish when we feel unheard. But setting our sights on God and his endless love diffuses the difficulty within.

As we try to decipher the messages others are sending, what is the message *we* want to send back? What does God want to share with the person we are responding to through our next steps?

Get rid of all bitterness, rage and anger, brawling and slander, along with every form of malice. Be kind and

compassionate to one another, forgiving each other,
just as in Christ God forgave you.

EPHESIANS 4:31-32

Forgiveness goes a long way, as does the tone with which we offer it. As God works his righteousness in us, we become vessels of righteousness to the people around us. As we are filled more and more with God's fullness, our inner knowledge of his love and the riches he offers us produces in us responses of grace, gentleness, wisdom, and love.

My dear brothers and sisters, take note of this: Every-
one should be quick to listen, slow to speak and slow to
become angry, because human anger does not produce
the righteousness that God desires.

JAMES 1:19-20

Empathetic listening sets us in the shoes of others, allowing us to hear where they are coming from and seek to understand why they are upset. We can take in their words and process them through the lens of love; we can have compassion for the hurt underneath their anger and recognize their great need for God's grace poured into their lives. We can pray for them to experience this love, and ask that it would transform their hearts and move our relationship with them toward unity. And we can stop the anger from seeping into our hearts, halting any rushed comment that might cripple our character.

If it is possible, as far as it depends on you, live at peace with everyone.

ROMANS 12:18

God knows the motivations of everyone, and it's up to him to deal with us all in our individual pieces. Live in peace as best you can, letting God work on how to handle your heart's response, and acting out of the overflow of his love and forgiveness. His heart is big enough to cover ours, and to create a little extra care for others when conflict comes.

REFLECT

How have you handled harsh words from others in the past? Have you gone to God to ask how to respond?

How can you extend God's grace to others in the middle of disagreement? What obstacles make it hard for you to do this?

LINGER

Matthew 5:9; Luke 6:27; Hebrews 12:14

RESPOND

Father, the strain of harsh words and unyielding rules to follow in some relationships is exhausting. I am tempted to snap a quick and smart response, but I know that isn't what you would want. Please help me see the grace you extend to me, and witness how your heart is always full of love. Let your grace and love transform me so I may give that grace and love to the ones who hurt me. In Jesus' name, amen.

PRAISE

"Jesus Paid It All" by Worship Circle

UP THE MOUNTAIN:

GOOD HARD THINGS

———

Our necks crane 90 degrees to take in the top of the mountain, a mere speck in the sky, past the clouds, up crags and rock, hewn hard spaces with little to no pathway. Somewhere beyond the typical 2,500-meter altitude mark, snow collects. How in the world can we make this trek from the lowest of lows to soaring heights? How can we adjust our breathing to manage this new elevation?

A move, a job change, a marriage, a baby, a promotion, the fulfillment of a dream. All these are good, blessings we hoped for that are worthy of celebrating. But these all can lead us into unknown seasons, wondering what is next, navigating the unacknowledged stress that creeps up the same as it does with harder transitions. These are times of spiritual growth, and we all know that with growth comes growing pains. It's a chance to know God in deeper ways, but often, our path forward isn't one we've previously explored, and it stretches our faith.

Belief can be an impossible mountain to scale. When we've lived in the valley so long, battled to keep our faith when past hardships have led us to distraction and doubt, sometimes it feels too hard to hope, to look to the Lord and seek his face, to say over and over to our hearts that he will come through.

This is exactly where God wants us to hold to belief because he still holds us. Even if we have faith the size of a minuscule mustard seed, we can still scale the enormous mountain before us. God wants to build our belief, brick by brick, if necessary, to get us to remember how he's moved in our lives before. From this remembrance, we take courage to believe that he will remain faithful in the good hard.

35

LIFE LOOKS DIFFERENT

Processing Transition

YESTERDAY AND TODAY AND
FOREVER. **HEBREWS 13:8**

In the span of three years, I got married, took a new job, moved with my husband into our first house (which needed a lot of work!), and then got a puppy one month after the move. To say I was hit with transition would be an understatement. I didn't include the medical situations that arose over those three years, because I wanted to focus on the good changes. Marrying the kindest, gentlest man was the greatest gift God could give me. Moving out of our cramped apartment on a busy downtown street and into a house we could call our own was another answered prayer. And making the quick, life-altering decision to drive five hours to Minnesota and pick up the most adorable rescue puppy changed our daily routine in the best of ways. But my goodness—so much change, in what felt like so little time! I needed to process even *one* of the changes in order to acclimate to my new life, but it seemed like every time I got to a point where I could begin to see where God was moving, another circumstance arose and I snapped my attention to the next thing in front of me with no time to properly breathe between transitions.

Any change, even something beautiful like getting married, landing that job you've always dreamed of, or moving out on your own for the first time, is going to bring up nerves as we face the unknown. We look for ways to navigate this new situation, and we search for assurance that our old life hasn't left us. When life looks different from what we've experienced, we search for familiar reminders of what once was that offer us comfort and affirmation.

Fortunately, God never leaves us to navigate life on our own. When we look back through the Bible on all the times he has led his people through transitions—new lands, new kings, building the church— he has provided for their needs every step of the way. His character remains true and unchanging, and when he promises to take us somewhere good, we can believe that he will see that promise through.

Here's the good promise he gives for us to hold to today: "Jesus Christ is the same yesterday and today and forever" (Hebrews 13:8).

Even if we're filled with trepidation about unpacking our new environment or grieving the good things we had to leave behind to make room for better things, we can remember how God has been with us before (Psalm 121:8), and how we've come through changed, softened, and stronger in faith. He has goodness in these good things, and even when we don't quite know how to handle them, he does. He will help walk us through this next season, even when our heads spin at the suddenness of the move or all the work that needs to be done before moving on.

Tell him how you're feeling about this new season. You may love a good change and long for more, or you may need a while to adjust to the idea of what's next, but in both cases, God wants to hear about how you feel. If you're excited, tell him. And if you're also a little sad, tell him. In whatever way this good change affects you, it's healing to let God into every stage of it.

We can take heart in a God who stays consistent. When everything around us seems to shift under our feet like plate tectonics, God's steadfast love keeps us standing.

Your word, L ORD, is eternal; it stands firm in the heavens.
Your faithfulness continues through all generations; you
established the earth, and it endures.

PSALM 119:89-90

In just a short time, our lives might look completely different from what we ever imagined. But with God, they are always good.

REFLECT

What was your most recent transition? Was it exciting or nerve-racking or both? What unexpected challenges did you face?

How does knowing that God does not change help you as you walk through this season?

LINGER

Lamentations 3:22-23; Psalm 136:1; 2 Thessalonians 3:5

RESPOND

Father, I'm in a season of change. While there's excitement within it, there is also nervousness because I don't know what it will be like. You are unchanging, and your faithfulness endures throughout all generations. Help me stand on your steadfastness, and walk with me into this newness so I may see where you are and all you want to do in it. In Jesus' name, amen.

PRAISE

"You Are Unchanging" by Sovereign Grace Music

36

BEGIN AGAIN

Recovering Hope for Fresh Starts

MAKING EVERYTHING NEW. **REVELATION 21:5**

Moving from a winter season of uncertainty, struggle, or disappointment and into the spring of our hearts can be challenging, even though more light is dawning, and hope has arrived and blooms fuller each day. When we've lived so long in shadow, stepping into the light can cause us to hesitate and overthink, unsure whether we are truly moving into something that promises life and joy. Believing that good is coming can be a slow and subtle process, one we don't recognize until one day we look back on where we've been and see how goodness has grown over time.

But God's patience persists through our hesitation. Do not underestimate the great work of our God: He makes all things new. He paves ways through the wilderness and brings streams into the desert (Isaiah 43:18-19). Where there was desolation, tender shoots spring up in restoration. Tears are wiped away, and we are held in the loving embrace of a good God who is sowing beauty back into our lives. From the ashes, dreams are reborn.

There will be an ultimate day when Jesus returns and reigns on earth as he restores it to the way all things were meant to be. He will bring justice and healing, and everything will be set right. We have this promise to look forward to (Revelation 21:6), but one more beautiful thing about God is that he is still setting things straight in the here and now.

He who was seated on the throne said,
"I am making everything new!"
REVELATION 21:5

Maybe you've lived in disappointment for too long as one dream after another broke and disbanded; God is shaping a new dream in you and building joy within. Maybe you've moved more times than you care to count and haven't found the deep and lasting connection you crave; this next move could be where God brings community like you've never imagined. Maybe it's been a long season of battling physical ailments and now you have a clean bill of health; what could God want to show you in this season of building strength and entering different daily rhythms?

Where we've been rundown, God is restoring. Jesus came not just to close the gap between God and humanity through his death on the cross, but to give us a glimpse of what kingdom living looks like when we walk with him.

The Spirit of the Sovereign LORD is on me, because the LORD has anointed me to proclaim good news to the poor. He has sent me to bind up the brokenhearted, to proclaim freedom for the captives and release from darkness for the prisoners, to proclaim the year of the LORD's favor and the day of vengeance of our God, to comfort all who mourn, and provide for those who grieve in Zion—to bestow on them a crown of beauty instead of ashes, the oil of joy instead of mourning, and a garment of praise instead of a spirit of despair. They will be called oaks of righteousness, a planting of the LORD for the display of his splendor (Isaiah 61:1-3).

This passage in Isaiah shows us how Jesus desires to work in the world. He has come to bind up the brokenhearted, to free those caught in captivity, to declare God's favor, and to comfort the weary. He longs to end our mourning by making joy pour from our hearts again, reversing the curse of death and decay and restoring all things bright and beautiful.

This is the hope we have as we tentatively place one foot and then the next onto the new path we are walking. He gives us assurance of his faithfulness as we begin again in a season of healing and newness. Jesus, who came to feel all we feel and live as we lived, cups our face in his hands and declares, "I am making all things new!"

Nothing is beyond his reach or attention. He is anointed to repair and renew, to weave a garment of praise and plant oaks of righteousness that display the splendor of the Lord. This means me; this means you.

Lift your eyes to Jesus and see him doing a new thing in you. Are you ready to begin again?

REFLECT

Where would you like God to give you beauty instead of ashes? How can you lift your eyes to see what Jesus is doing in and around you?

Are you ready to begin again? What fears or obstacles might

keep you from believing in the good things God is preparing for you?

LINGER

Isaiah 43:18-19; 2 Corinthians 5:17; Revelation 21:4

RESPOND

Lord, I have lingered in the ashes too long. A new day is dawning, and I see you moving me into a season of light and hope. Thank you for being with me through it all. Thank you that nothing is beyond your reach, and you are bringing beauty for those ashes. Make a new way in me as I begin again. Give me confidence to believe in the good you are bringing and the love you have already provided. In Jesus' name, amen.

PRAISE

"Good Things" by MacKenzie Walker, Luis Vicens, and SEU Worship

37

GRACE AND GRIT

Coping with (Good) Change

MIGHTY WARRIOR. **JUDGES 6:12**

It was a new responsibility, and I had absolutely no idea what I was doing. In the span of six days, Eric and I had seen a rescue page with a picture of a sweet "Beaglier" puppy (a mix between a beagle and Cavalier King Charles spaniel), filled out an application, talked with one of the staff, and driven five hours up to Minnesota to bring our 4.6-pound Alfie home with us. After the initial shine and awe of bringing a living thing into our lives had faded, the reality of raising a puppy struck, and I was paralyzed with all the second-guessing, doubt, and overwhelm.

What did we just do? I wondered four days later as this soft chestnut and white pup with floppy ears and melt-your-heart eyes lay curled sleeping on my lap. By adopting this puppy, we'd also adopted nights of disrupted sleep, the constant vigilance of housebreaking, and work schedules that suddenly collided with the unknown rhythm of attending to Alfie during the day.

I know adopting a puppy is a pretty ordinary change that didn't truly threaten my way of life, and I also know that the period of difficulty we navigated was relatively short in the scheme of things. But in that period of my life, it was a major disruption to the routine I was used to! I wrestled with guilt that I couldn't handle it all, and feared we would never find a new normal. This beautiful puppy enhanced our lives, but how would we *live* as a family of three?

The answer? With grace and grit. Grace to make mistakes and learn as we went, and to see God's love in a new way through this squiggly, happy puppy. Grit that built our character and faith as Eric and I leaned on one another and the Lord to make it through each stage dog experts map out: the first three days, three weeks, three months. Eventually, we got the hang of this new homelife, and the more things calmed down in our days, the more we recognized how God's care and presence had guided us along the way.

No matter where you find yourself right now, God will give you grace and strength for each new season. He knows exactly what you need at this time, how you need it, and when.

Let's look to Scripture's account of Gideon to see a biblical example of short-term hardship. A young man from a small and seemingly insignificant clan of Israel encountered the Lord, who set him on a new path that had greater purpose than he ever could have imagined. Oppressed by the Midianites, the Israelites sought shelter in caves and hid their crops. They had been disobedient to God and worshipped idols, and now lived hidden and in fear, oppressed and on the run.

But God, in his great grace and compassion, still had plans for his people. Young and inexperienced Gideon was threshing wheat when the angel of the Lord came to him with quite the greeting: "The LORD is with you, mighty warrior" (Judges 6:12).

God called him by a new moniker, one he knew Gideon would grow into: *mighty warrior*. Here was the youngest member of the weakest clan in the region, and God was calling him mighty? Gideon wrestled with who he was according to generational standing, but God saw something coming that Gideon could never anticipate. He charged him with leading Israel and defeating their enemy, the Midianites. The Israelites' suffering had a time limit, and their days of hiding were almost done.

When Gideon answered the Lord with a hopeless and helpless response, how did God reply? "The LORD answered, 'I will be with you, and you will strike down all the Midianites'" (Judges 6:16).

Gideon still wrestled with understanding his identity and accepting that God was choosing him for something longed for by his people, but he eventually embraced God's invitation and stepped out into a difficult but worthy calling. God gave him the grace to see himself how God saw him, and the grit to persevere through a grueling process of determining who would be part of the army and preparing for battle.

God's presence sustained Gideon, and it sustains us today through whatever we walk through. He equipped my family to endure what felt like the never-ending puppy stage, and revealed some of his unconditional love to us through the way Alfie loves us. God's presence gives each of us power and proper perspective, enabling us to walk into any battle we face because we trust him with the outcome. In all things, God gives us grace to greet our new endeavor, and grit to step into it with trust in the one who leads and loves us.

REFLECT

How have you been overwhelmed and in disbelief God could change your situation? How has he come through for you in past hardships?

Where do you most see God's presence right now, and what do you think he wants to do there?

LINGER

Exodus 33:14; Judges 6; Matthew 19:26

RESPOND

Lord, I thank you for this season I'm in. Even though it feels a bit overwhelming because I've never been here before, I know you go here with me, and you call me your loved one. May I live out my belovedness with grace and grit through the trust I have in you. In Jesus' name, amen.

PRAISE

"Champion" by Maverick City Music and UPPERROOM

38

REBUILDING

Staying Patient Through Unfinished Work

I AM WITH YOU. **HAGGAI 1:13**

Dirt.

Everywhere.

Dry, chalky dirt, swirling and hovering in the air, lifted high by the cars that maneuver around potholes and piles of gravel. When I take Alfie for his walk and his paws hit the grass, poofs of yellow dirt rise like steam.

For five months, our street has been in the process of renovation: new sewer lines, updated gas lines, the entire street made narrower to give room for a few extra feet of grass for the trees growing close to the asphalt. Our road has been in shambles, ripped up and with the underside of street exposed. Trucks, excavators, and construction workers have been outside our house most hours of the day, and a portable toilet has been on full display as it makes its way across neighbors' yards to follow the workers. Asphalt drilling starts at 7 a.m. to push dirt into mountains along the neighborhood until 7 p.m., and construction vehicles have parked across our driveway and blocked us in for an hour or two at a time. There has been constant chaos from when I wake up to well into the evening.

But now, construction seems to have ceased for the moment. The last few weeks have been quieter as the construction crew switched gears to focus on another street. Our street feels like it needs a haz-ard warning, asphalt torn up and covered with dirt, pavement pulled apart and trampled, exposed down to the bones. At this point, things will be left this way for who knows how long, everything everywhere until the team decides to tend to it again.

Does this scene not remind us of the mess of our lives, our circum-stances? Inconveniently jackhammered up, broken open, undersides exposed? Dust in our hair, our eyes, our hands. All the loud work of getting us in this fragile, precarious state, primed for restoration, and then suddenly silence, leaving us in a state of disarray seemingly with-out an end point.

Will we always be stuck like this? Where is God, and what is his plan? Has he left us to go and deal with something else, while we remain here, in the middle of the rubble of our lives?

We wonder, *is he just going to leave us in this mess? Will this work be finished? Will there be answers to our prayers, and will rebuilt lives put wind in our sails once again?*

Sometimes our lives may seem messier than usual, but they will not always be this way.

The Israelites felt this plight too. When they were taken captive by the Babylonians, their precious temple was destroyed, flattened, walls torn to rubble. After 70 years of exile, they finally made it back home to Israel. But they had work to do, and it would take time, money, and focus. They were hesitant to start, knowing if they began in the mid-dle, a lot could go wrong. So they waited, living quiet lives in a city with shaky protection and a less-than-spectacular temple.

Eventually, vision was given and implemented for the temple's reconstruction. And after that, a cupbearer named Nehemiah was plucked from the palace and burdened with the task of arranging the rebuilding of the city's walls (Nehemiah 1–2). It would be hard work, full of manual labor, political opposition, and testing of faith. But both teams didn't go at it alone.

> Haggai, the LORD's messenger, gave this message of the LORD to the people: "I am with you," declares the LORD. So the LORD stirred up the spirit of Zerubbabel son of Shealtiel, governor of Judah, and the spirit of Joshua son of Jozadak, the high priest, and the spirit of the whole remnant of the people. They came and began to work on the house of the LORD Almighty, their God, on the twenty-fourth day of the sixth month (Haggai 1:13-15).

The Lord was with his people, and he enabled them to do the work he'd called them to while providing them with the resources needed.

God is with us in the middle of our mess, enabling us to continue through. He has already seen what the end will be, so we can trust each step he calls us to take as we follow him. If we don't see a way, he is making a way. If we don't feel like we have the resources to maintain, he is the owner of cattle on a thousand hills (Psalm 50:10)—his resources are abundant, and he is generous. He provides what we need, in the exact way that we need it, at the right time for us to receive it.

Amid the mess of renovation, life continues. And in the meantime, we get an opportunity to know God better, see him for who he is, and watch his work unfold in and around us.

Like my street, the construction of our lives has a completion date. We can rest in that, enduring the dirt and the temporary unraveled nature of our lives because we know that the experience is refining us and giving us a new way to build our faith.

Entrust the work of your heart to God. It will all be put back together.

REFLECT

What is the mess of your life right now? Is it a situation that doesn't seem solvable? Is it a heart posture that has left you in the wrong position?

Will you allow God to excavate and dig in this mess, believing that even though it looks rough, he will bring it all together? Ask him to give you the patience and continued hope you need today.

LINGER

Nehemiah 6:9; Joel 2:25-26; Jeremiah 29:10-14

RESPOND

Father, the state of my life looks a little messy at the moment. I feel like so much has been torn up, and there is no indication of when things will be put back together. Will you give me your eyes to see where you are at work, and to trust that you will be with me as this excavation continues? Help me trust that you know what you are doing, and all will come together as it should. In Jesus' name, amen.

PRAISE

"God Turn It Around" by Church of the City and Jon Reddick

39

THE HEART'S QUIET HUMBLING

Drawing Close When We'd Rather Hide

CALMED AND QUIETED. **PSALM 131:2**

When God wants our attention, he'll be sure to get it.

He wanted mine the other day. I knew it too. I needed to come to him about a difficult issue regarding a close relationship, but I tend to stuff down this kind of discomfort and put off those hard conversations with God, *especially* when they relate to the matters of my heart. All morning, I had this knowledge pressing on my heart, and as I came back to work from lunch, car idling in the parking lot as I watched the flag across the street flutter in the wind, I knew we *would* have a discussion. Just not now. I had too much to do and too much on my mind, diving headlong into a job I loved, thinking about current writing projects that excited me, and preparing ways I could encourage my family when I stopped by in the evening.

The rest of the afternoon passed quickly. The quick hello I'd planned to say to my parents and little brother turned into a visit that led me to stay later than I'd intended, warming myself in the comfort of the home where I grew up. By the time I ran a few errands and made it back home, it was nine in the evening. I had hoped I could somehow avoid that pressing conversation by keeping myself away so late, but as soon as I hung up my coat, switched on the living room lights, and entered my bedroom, I felt him watching me, waiting with words unspoken, like he always does.

I was cowering and I knew it. So I continued to stall, picking up my room, checking my email, hopping in the shower. Still, my heart felt God's gentle pressure, and still, I padded once again around my room, shifting my sheets, examining the ceiling fan. Minutes later, I was still pacing, but now my heart beat wildly within me. This time, I knew my fight was over.

The room was silent, but my mind was racing, running like a horse around and around a track. I couldn't think of a starting point and felt lost trying even to begin my prayer, so I did what comes the most naturally to me: I grabbed my black leather journal and penned my request to God.

Why do we avoid going to God when he's the one who knows our hearts best? When he's the one who carefully crafted us in the secret place (Psalm 139:15) and holds us close to his chest in comfort? We flail and fight and distance ourselves from him when we need to do the exact opposite. We allow ourselves to get so caught up in the good things of life that we forget the better: being with our God and growing in intimacy with him.

When we think of hiding from God, we might think about the prophet Jonah, who was so keen to avoid God's commands that he set out in the opposite direction of where God had told him to go, as if he believed he was capable of fleeing from God and his directions (Jonah 1). *I'd never disobey God like that*, we might think, and that may be true. But what about Martha, who kept herself so busy running around and taking care of all the good things in her household that she forgot the importance of falling at the feet of Jesus? (Luke 10:38-41). Are we ever guilty of using worthwhile work as a barrier between our hearts and God?

"Martha, Martha," the Lord answered, "you are worried and upset about many things, but few things are needed— or indeed only one. Mary has chosen what is better, and it will not be taken away from her."

LUKE 10:41-42

God longs for us to be still, surrender, and come close. Sometimes he makes our need to do this excruciatingly obvious, and other times he waits until we've expelled all our energy and worn ourselves out, so we have nothing left *but* to fall into him.

When our heart posture aligns with his, beautiful moments of relationship arise. But we must first be open and willing to hear from him, even when it comes as a quiet humbling of heart.

My heart is not proud, LORD, my eyes are not haughty; I do not concern myself with great matters or things too wonderful for me. But I have calmed and quieted myself; I am like a weaned child with its mother; like a weaned child I am content. Israel, put your hope in the LORD both now and forevermore.

PSALM 131

These three short verses that make up the entirety of Psalm 131 quickly readjust our hearts. God is patient and trustworthy, faithful from beginning to end, but he won't compete for our attention. In him we have our hope; we can choose to believe our tender spots and vulnerable places are safe with him. We should take comfort in the promise that his perfect love always casts away our fear (1 John 4:18).

As I poured out my prayers in my journal and repeated this psalm to myself, my heart calmed down and found rest in the God who knows its every beat. We talked, and my chest lightened as I unloaded to my great Advocate. This can be our rhythm: to still and quiet ourselves before our dear and patient God. He knows how we hide, how we avoid how we feel, how the storms rage within, and how, even with the best intentions, our affection can drift as we set our sights on the things of this world. But when we realign our hearts and tune our ears to hear what he whispers, he will raise us to new heights, pour peace into our weary and ragged souls, and keep our attention fixed where it belongs. How comforting it is to climb into the lap of our great God and rest a while! His presence is our prize as we quiet our souls and place our hope in him.

REFLECT

Have you been so caught up in the daily grind of good work that you've forgotten—or avoided—being still with God? What might he want to say to you that you haven't made time to hear?

Take a few minutes and be still with him. What has kept you distracted? What has made you wary of drawing closer in prayer? What's on your heart that you need to share with God?

LINGER

Proverbs 15:33; Micah 6:8; James 4:6

RESPOND

Lord, you are my great love. I try to hide my heart from you, but you already know it, and you still want me to come close. I want to rest with you; come and share what is on my mind. I can come to you with everything. How beautiful you are, how gently you rock me in your arms, stilling my anxiety and soothing me as your child. Let me take refuge in you, to quiet myself in order to hear your whisper. In Jesus' name, amen.

PRAISE

"Rest" by Leanna Crawford

40

SOMEWHERE NEW

Facing the Unknown

HOW WE KNOW. **1 JOHN 5:2**

January 2013

It seemed like an incredible opportunity: a position as a writer for an international ministry. I was familiar and involved with the Fellowship of Christian Athletes as a high school and college athlete, and I was well versed and supportive of their mission. I had even written a few devotions for them and given an interview that was featured in their magazine. At this time in my life, I needed to shift directions and felt God leading me into writing and ministry. When FCA came to mind and I visited their website, seeing the available position of content writer felt like the answer to a prayer. When I was offered the job, there was only one catch: its location in Kansas City, 574 miles away from my home in Wisconsin. I had never lived outside my county before, and now I had the choice to leave my family, my friends, my church—everything I knew—and venture into a complete unknown.

What to do? I played out scenarios in my mind, until one day, when I was mid-flight on a plane over the Rockies, I knew in my gut that I would choose this new job in this new city. And wasn't that what I ultimately wanted? To grow in deeper living with the Lord, to be challenged in my faith and experience the things I needed in order to grow?

So I said yes, packed up my belongings, said goodbye to my beloved family, and drove eight and a half hours to a new life in Kansas City.

Moves are hard. Moves matter. We move away from lives we've known, people we love; we leave familiar places and comfortable ways of being. But we have a chance to build new experiences in places that are different but have potential to house beautiful seasons that we never envisioned.

It takes courage to step from one setting into another. A new job, a new place of residence, life in a new state or country. And like Abram setting out from Ur, we can often have limited knowledge of what lays before us and little directive.

> The Lord had said to Abram, "Go from your country, your people and your father's household to the land I will show you. I will make you into a great nation, and I will bless you; I will make your name great, and you will be a blessing. I will bless those who bless you, and whoever curses you I will curse; and all peoples on earth will be blessed through you." So Abram went, as the Lord had told him (Genesis 12:1-4).

Sometimes God asks us to go to places we would never have considered on our own. Sometimes the reasons are obvious, and sometimes the reasons are unclear. But either way, at the heart of a call to begin a new journey, we ask ourselves what God is inviting us into, and whether we will respond by following him.

As we consider the decisions before us, let us keep in mind what God has for us within these choices, and why.

This is how we know that we love the children of God:
by loving God and carrying out his commands.
In fact, this is love for God: to keep his commands.
And his commands are not burdensome.

1 JOHN 5:2-3

Greater strength begins with obedience. It should be a joy to go where God leads, to look for each next step as a window where we get to witness more of God's character and heart toward us. As we grow in spiritual depth and experience, our exercised faith gives further grace, allowing us to live a life worthy of our calling that pleases God and grows fruit from our choices and heart posture (Colossians 1:10).

We love God by keeping his commands and by looking to him for direction and discernment. God's invitations offer life, grace, and goodness. They are not burdensome, nor are they meant to weigh us down or provoke us to anxiety in deliberation. Quite the opposite.

Moves come once in a while, but how we respond to the thousands of choices we encounter every day says just as much about the state of our spirit and where our allegiance lies. Goodbyes to an old way of life lead into new opportunities to connect with God through a greater experiential relationship with Jesus (2 Corinthians 5:17).

Say yes to God. However he is calling to you, whatever the invitation. He may be moving you somewhere that might not yet be fully revealed, but you can trust that his heart within it is for your good and growth (Psalm 145:9).

REFLECT

Have you gone through a big move, either literally or metaphorically? Where did you see God in the decision?

In what ways is God growing you through transitions into an unknown?

LINGER

2 Corinthians 1:20; Ephesians 4:22-24; 1 Peter 1:14-16

RESPOND

Father, it can be hard to leave what I know to follow you. I've been comfortable, and I've liked this predictable life. But I sense you calling out to me, inviting me deeper into your mystery and asking me to say yes to this adventure with you. Strengthen my heart and trust as I take a step in faith to follow where you lead. In Jesus' name, amen.

PRAISE

"I Will Follow" by Chris Tomlin

41

NEXT STEPS

Giving God Control of Our Plans

ESTABLISHES THEIR STEPS. **PROVERBS 16:9**

In the summer of 2020, I was fresh off my little wedding and beginning life with Eric. A month after we were married, I left my job directing a nonprofit student center. I had felt burned out and been burdened by a desire for something different, but I wasn't quite sure where that *different* would lead. Eric graciously advised me to step away from my current role and lean into what I truly loved: writing. So I began to put my feelers out for freelance work, praying for discernment and direction in the meantime. It was a daunting task; I was moving into a new season that both excited and scared me. Where would I end up? Would this pursuit of my dream just be a fun but temporary exploration? And why was international communications continuing to pop up to the top of my heart?

I ventured into the unknown, and the odds seemed more against me than for me. But Eric and I trusted that God was indeed inviting me into *something*, so I wanted to find out what that was, without panicking about having enough income to help with the rent and living expenses or whether I would land on my feet. What was coming? I strained and struggled to see ahead into what was not yet clear.

Think about those times when you've stood on the precipice of what has been and what is to come. How did this make you feel? Were you anxious or excited? Did you roll with the outcome or attempt to take action by coming up with a plan?

Whether the pull of something that's coming gives you energy or drains you, the entrance into this new season starts with seeking God. He's seen us through every path we've walked already, and he won't leave us to figure this one out on our own.

I will instruct you and teach you in the way you should go;
I will counsel you with my loving eye on you.

PSALM 32:8

We want what's best, and what's best is what God has in store. Remember, his heart for us is always good, and he wants to transform our own hearts to more closely resemble the image of his Son, Jesus. This involves dusting away any pride that's settled upon us. Heading into the unknown shakes us, allowing any fear, unbelief, anger, or stubbornness to rise to the surface, and giving God the opportunity to tend to what is holding us back from desiring his best.

Even with good options on the horizon, we can try to take on too much in the name of moving things to fit where they "should" go. We can write out a detailed plan with each step clearly outlined, and we might even allow ourselves to believe we have the power to follow each step perfectly. But while plans can be helpful to a degree, is that where God will truly meet us?

In their hearts humans plan their course,
but the LORD *establishes their steps.*

PROVERBS 16:9

It isn't bad to be prepared or discerning about the next thing, but when we try to take matters into our own hands, it's like having some pieces of a puzzle we don't have the full picture of. We try to assemble the pieces, even when some of them don't seem to fit together. We twist and push them into place, trying to make up for the pieces we're missing. The more we try to force things, the more distorted the picture becomes. But when we hand the pieces to God and let him arrange them, knowing he sees the ultimate picture and the best way to put the puzzle together, we take the pressure and striving off our own shoulders and rest instead on the mighty wisdom and ability of our God.

We can say with confidence, "He is establishing my steps." And we can believe it.

Think about Moses as we meet him in Exodus 3. Did he want to stop being a shepherd living a quiet life in Midian to lead the charge to take God's people out of slavery? He didn't know what was ahead—the long days, the grumbling crowds, the force of Pharaoh—but he knew who would lead him through.

After about ten months of freelance and contract work, I landed with the global sports ministry where I had worked years before, but this time in a new position. One that would serve our leaders around the US and the world through capturing and sharing their stories. The cries of my heart were answered in ways I never saw coming. God came through, even more than I could have pictured. I had hoped the course in my heart would lead me here, but God determined the steps that would guide me to arrive when and where he needed me to.

We can rest in the assurance that our great God knows what is for our good. We can't mess up his plan for us. He is taking great care in keeping us on his course. We can make plans all we want, but it's God who determines our steps. Why would we want it any other way?

REFLECT

Are you in a season of transition? What has been exciting about this time, and what has been difficult?

Where can you invite God into your hopes and plans for what's next, and trust him with the outcome?

LINGER

Exodus 3:9-10; Proverbs 20:24; James 1:5-6

RESPOND

Oh Lord, it's hard to go into the unknown, even when I'm hopeful. I have so many ideas about where I want to go, but help me pause and let you into the process. You are wise, you are loving, and you know what is best for me. You have my good in mind and I believe you will see me through to this next season. Thank you for being loving and intentional. In Jesus' name, amen.

PRAISE

"Waymaker" by Michael W. Smith

42

GOD FOR ALL SEASONS

Embracing Transition

I THE LORD. **MALACHI 3:6**

Since the calendar turned to September, our Wisconsin weather has shifted too. Cool, crisp, dew-drenched mornings now burn off into a manageable warmth, tinting oak leaves gold and burnt orange at the edges. Birdsong has seemingly multiplied, and a natural slowness has set in that helps my heart better absorb the days. Autumn is coming, pieces of it already evident.

Inevitably, the passage of days gives way to the next stage of the year, the order of the world around me changing its attire. Seasons blend. We leave one behind and enter another. We may be sad to see one season end, knowing we'll miss the blooms of spring, the sunshine of summer, the vibrancy of fall, or the coziness of winter, but we can't hold on to one piece of time as it fades away; we can only keep moving forward. This is the way of things. It is the way of our own lives too.

We experience seasons of transitions—new jobs, friendships, moves, movements in our hearts—and somewhere along the way, we must leave room to receive change. Going into something new while leaving what's familiar behind can fill us with hesitation, sadness, and a desire to hold on to something that may just be keeping us back. To experience what God has prepared for us, let's loosen our grip on the way things have been and look into the new experiences that have been created for us.

Forget the former things; do not dwell on the past.
See, I am doing a new thing!
Now it springs up; do you not perceive it? I am making a
way in the wilderness and streams in the wasteland.
ISAIAH 43:18-19

Yes, it can be—and oftentimes *is*—scary to step where we've never been before. Change comes with its own set of circumstances, rhythms to learn, and a period of settling in. It can throw us off our nicely arranged routine and order, but take heart—the one who goes with you is well versed in what's ahead. God knows the beginning from the end (Isaiah 46:10). He is sure, steadfast, and knowledgeable. He has a plan of which he knows every angle. And while the environment around us might look different, or while we may have to take the scary first step of finding new friends as we navigate new territory, we have a God who stays the same while also staying with us.

I the Lord do not change.
MALACHI 3:6

God's unchangeable character strengthens our hearts. He is our God for all seasons, no matter where we find ourselves. He is all-knowing, always present, wise, compassionate, secure, and strong.

When we feel unsteady in our own seasons of transition, we can stand on the promises of God our Provider and Sustainer. He *is* certain, and when our trust is set in him, we begin to believe that where we are journeying may just become a beautiful place of our beginning.

When we have the loving guidance of the God who has already gone before us and understands our concerns, we don't need to hold so tightly to the way of what was. We can take comfort that he reassures with his presence while we walk into what's next.

Embrace the shift of seasons, remember what was good, and believe there will be something even better. Because with God, our rock and anchor, we already have a place to put our hope as we go, no matter the season.

REFLECT

What season do you find yourself in right now? How can you remind yourself of God's steadfastness in this season?

Which of God's characteristics do you need to focus on (faithful, compassionate, trustworthy, and others)? What can you do to form a habit of remembering those characteristics?

LINGER

Psalm 20:7; 2 Timothy 4:18; 1 John 5:14

RESPOND

Lord, you know that the seasons and transitions of life can be hard for me. Things happen that I'm not ready for, and even when they are good things, they still bring a period of adjustment. May I hold to your truths, especially the truth that you do not change. You stay the same, and you stay with me. Help me live out of an overflow of trust that you will see me through this season. In Jesus' name, amen.

PRAISE

"Take You at Your Word" by Benjamin William Hastings and Cody Carnes

THROUGH THE NIGHT, INTO MORNING:

GREAT IS HIS FAITHFULNESS

—

Has the sky always looked this bright? The clouds so touchable? The scent of sweetgrass, lavender, and spearmint is in the air, dancing. Light plays off the pond, the clean, fresh newness that comes after rain, covering the land with life; the rolling hills, supple woods and painted horizon teem with it.

Have we made it through? We have found where we are meant to be for now, after wandering through the forests and embankments to finally stand and scan with our renewed eyes the crest of crags from this observation point. Here, beauty abounds.

We breathe in the healing roll of air in our lungs, a reprieve and reminder of Eden.

We chose to believe, and look how God has responded, all he has given and done. Look at where he has brought us: through incredible health challenges, dangerous darkness and mental anguish, unraveled relationships, and heart-withering loneliness. And how has God's faithfulness seen us through? Oh, let us count the ways.

Here is where we pile our remembrance stones, stack them one on top of the other, souvenirs from along the way that take us back to each place we've been. Reminders of his faithfulness to see us through the deep shadows of anxiety, torrents of fear, darkness of loneliness, relentlessness of sickness, and everything in between.

We see his heartbeats behind every bush, burning with his presence, every valley holy.

Oh wonder, our God has been good.

43

A SEASON OF SUN

Finding Joy Again

YOUR LIGHT HAS COME. **ISAIAH 60:1**

Sun streaks in from the cracks in my curtains, ushering in the day. I stir, roll under the covers, waking. The warmth of the morning heightens as I pull back the curtains and reveal an impossibly bright day. Or maybe that's just the way I see it, the way it feels, as I notice the bubble of hope in my chest slowly expanding.

After years of darkness weighing me down as I struggled with physical and mental health, during these last five months I've noticed a slow dissipation of the dense fog shrouding my mind, a gradual lifting of the albatross that had been upon me.

Is this what it means when the goodness of God marks seasons in due time? When the one who has allowed the night now lets the light in?

Arise, shine, for your light has come,
and the glory of the LORD rises upon you.

ISAIAH 60:1

He who made the moon and marked it for the night also made the sun blaze and bring the day, his presence enduring during both

(Psalm 104:19-23). He is as present in the dark as he is in the day, even though we may feel like he has hidden himself from our sight. But if he says he is with us, he is with us, and we hold to the truth of his Word in the night until we can look upon him when daylight streams in.

Remember the treasures found in darkness, yes. But when the sun appears and your heart is alive, rejoice.

Pause for a moment. Take a slow breath, hold it, and exhale. Do it again. Now, look back. See where God has taken you. Through the struggle. Through the valley. Through the uncertainty, the strain, the heartache, and hesitations. He was *there*, through it all. *In* it all. Never once did his eyes stray or his attention fall from you. For he is a faithful God, forever attentive and full of grace.

Those nights of unending darkness when you couldn't see how you'd come out on the other side? Now day is dawning, and all the Lord sees is light.

Even the darkness will not be dark to you;
the night will shine like the day,
for darkness is as light to you.

PSALM 139:12

The crushing weight of disappointment and loneliness that threatened to take your joy? See how secure your hope and joy are when held up to the strength of our Savior.

Do not grieve, for the joy of the LORD is your strength.
NEHEMIAH 8:10

Remember how God has carried you when you couldn't take another step. Notice the manna he provided each day, the streams formed in the desert (Isaiah 43:19). He made a way when no way was found (Isaiah 43:16), and we have found him worthy.

He delights in you, his child, He knows the paths you've journeyed, the sacrifice and suffering it's taken. But see how he has guided and watched over you. Good Shepherd that he is, his heart has always been for you to come close, to lean on him and rely on his provision. Trust is built through burden, and you are better for it. The battles you've endured, you have not endured alone.

This is our triumph, our song of praise: The God of our lives has led us through the valley, and we are still standing. Do you see the wonders he has done on our behalf?

From promises stamped in the beginning of time to their fulfillment in the life, death, and resurrection of Jesus, God is a God who keeps his word.

He won't ever stop providing a way forward for us. He won't ever stop providing a lantern for our steps, lighting up our path toward his goodness (Psalm 119:105). Swing wide the curtains of your heart. Can you see the sun?

REFLECT

Where have you noticed God's goodness in your life?

How does it give you comfort to know that darkness isn't dark to God? Praise the God who brought you out of the valley, and tell others about what he has done.

LINGER

Psalm 84:11; Psalm 113:3; Ecclesiastes 11:7

RESPOND

Oh Lord, I have lived in the darkness for so long. Now I begin to see rays of sun fill my heart. Thank you that you are the God of light and dark, and that you have never left me alone at any time. Thank you for bringing sun to my spirit, and reminding me of your faithfulness to bring me through. In Jesus' name, amen.

PRAISE

"Faithful God" by I AM THEY

44

THIS IS THE WONDER

Receiving God's Abundance

YOU ALSO WILL LIVE. **JOHN 14:19**

Spring makes its way into the earth and my heart. Blossoms budding after a long winter's sleep. Color begins to burst, shattering the monochrome with rainbow arrangements of lilies, tulips, and daffodils. Sun is seen beyond the covering of clouds; they clear away and reveal bright smiling skies. There is hope for the next season, a way out of the endless cold and long stretch of night. All around us, life springs forth, from the grass growing green to the spindly frames of fawns peeking from bushes. Beauty seen, beauty experienced, and a bright joy that rises within us at the signs of lighter days.

What a gift, the changing of seasons, balm for our weary bodies and minds when we think we can't take one more day in the grit of gray living.

We are offered life.

We are offered deeper life when we see the glory of the Lord arise around us. For he has given us everything we need to go from dull and drained to Technicolor living, hope in full, joy complete. Our true life always begins in Christ.

Because I live, you also will live.

JOHN 14:19

This is the wonder: that we can be with God forever and are made righteous through the blood of Jesus. It takes nothing for us to surrender our hearts to the one who has been faithful and true throughout the ages, but it took everything for Jesus to offer us this gracious gift.

Life in Christ is even more than we could imagine. He has pursued us. He has sustained us. He has taught us how to see him even in difficult circumstances. And he has set our faith on a firm foundation.

This is the power that now resides in us, the strength that carries us each day and comforts us each night. The one who rebuked the waves of the sea (Mark 4:39) can certainly still the storms within our days.

We get to be close to his heart, get to learn what he loves and do what is pleasing to him. We get to have our hearts overflow with his hope by the power of his Spirit so a weary world may be refreshed by him too (Romans 15:13).

It's the most marvelous thing, life in Christ. We get his presence from the Holy Spirit who dwells in us as believers. We have the love of the Father. We are never alone.

Christ came to give us life in full, and nothing else will satisfy (John 10:10). What we long for is found in Jesus. All answers are yes and amen in him (2 Corinthians 1:20).

When you feel unseen—God has never taken his eyes off you (Psalm 33:18).

When you feel directionless—God has good plans for you (Jeremiah 29:11).

When you feel disappointed—God will never let you down (Deuteronomy 31:8).

God is faithful to you. Again and again. This isn't a one-time thing, but a constant outpouring of his presence, goodness, and grace. In

Jesus, we are more than conquerors (Romans 8:37) and no good thing will he withhold to those who love him (Psalm 84:11).

He always finds us right where we need him. And, as always, I need him here in the tentative unfurling of hope. I need his peace that surpasses everything (Philippians 4:7). I need his guidance and discernment. But most of all, I just need him close. With me.

He is with us, always.

Go into today with your head held high—the God of the universe knows and loves you, and the same power that raised Christ from the dead resides in you (Romans 8:11). What a thought!

REFLECT

Are you in need of the season of spring in your soul? What would that look like?

How can you live out the abundant life Jesus offers you?

LINGER

Isaiah 58:11; 1 Corinthians 1:30; 1 Peter 2:24

RESPOND

Father, you are making a way for new life within me. It's been a long winter, but the ice of my heart is thawing, and I am recognizing your light around me. Thank you for the new life you promise through Christ. I want to receive what he offers and give my life over to his leading. God of comfort, you are grace-filled, and I am grateful. Help me to live in your life and love today and always. In Jesus' name, amen.

PRAISE

"Altar (Live)" by SEU Worship

45

SAFE WITH HIM

Being Vulnerable with God

IT'S GOOD TO BE NEAR GOD. **PSALM 73:28**

It's a dance of head and heart. We know we are safe with certain people, but our past makes us think of what has happened to us before, and we are tempted to believe the past will repeat itself. Even if those closest to you have been a steady and secure presence, at some point, they have said or done something to disappoint. They've broken your heart and been unavailable.

But not God. He is the *only* one who has never left us stranded or caused us to doubt his allegiance. In his presence is our peace (Ephesians 2:14), and it's wise to saturate our hearts with his steadfast love.

We can lean away from those who seek to find a close place in our hearts, afraid of getting hurt. But God implores us to come close, to lean in and learn who he is and the truth of his heart. He has wiped away our offenses and longs for us to return to his embrace (Isaiah 44:22).

I can be the most skittish of all, always guarding my tender heart. But I have experienced too much in the last few years to go anywhere other than into God's arms. The one who sees my experiences and stays with me is one worthy of my praise. He is trustworthy, he is strong, and he alone can save.

I am always with you; you hold me by my right hand.
You guide me with your counsel, and afterward you will
take me into glory. Whom have I in heaven but you?
And earth has nothing I desire besides you. My flesh and
my heart may fail, but God is the strength of my heart
and my portion forever.

PSALM 73:23-26

God is always with us, holding us by our hands. He guides us, consoles us, and sticks by us through our sorrow and surprise. We may lose a job, a loved one, a dream, or a piece of ourselves over the years, but he remains and offers us so much more than we could have imagined. There is nothing on this earth that can come close to what God gives.

When we are weak, his strength sustains.

When we are lacking, his grace provides.

When we are up against an impossibility, he does the unimagined (Matthew 19:26).

Plenty is his portion; salvation is his sweet spot.

As for me, it is good to be near God. I have made the
Sovereign LORD my refuge;
I will tell of all your deeds.

PSALM 73:28

It is good to be near my God.

Yes, it is good to walk entwined with him, his scent familiar, the cadence of his voice one we tune our ears to hear, *expect* to hear, and learn the fall of his footsteps so we can follow closely.

The closer we come to Jesus, the more secure we are. The more comforted we are. The more our confidence is cemented and our faith solidified. Sure, there will still be mysteries and mundane moments in life, but God with us makes them bearable. And not just bearable—in him we can be *in* these moments with an overcoming peace, well-watered joy, and enduring perseverance, with eyes that see his way through in it all.

When we make the Lord our refuge, we can let our guard down and relax our hearts, knowing we are never alone.

Let his banner over you be love (Song of Solomon 2:4), and the vastness of his presence be enough. He *is* more than enough; he is everything.

REFLECT

Where have you seen God stand by you when no one else has?

How can you invite God to come even closer to your heart today?

LINGER

Psalm 103:1; Jeremiah 23:24; Acts 17:27

RESPOND

Lord, thank you for being a constant in my life, especially in the times when nothing else has been. Thank you for being

*with me, for seeing me and loving me so well. I want to come
even closer to you, let you into the corners of my heart that I've
had a hard time sharing. Be gentle with me as I come close. It
is good to be near you. In Jesus' name, amen.*

PRAISE

"Make Room" by The Church Will Sing

46

IS IT OKAY TO BE HAPPY?

Experiencing God's Goodness

SEE THE GOODNESS. **PSALM 27:13-14**

Laughter. Lightheartedness. Joy that ripples through in my heart. How foreign they have been to me. How good they feel now. I remember standing in my kitchen amazed at the wonder of my life and asking God in my heart, *Is it okay to be happy?*

How heavy the seasons have been. How steadfast my God has stayed in them. Through the valley, the endless night, the worry and wondering and wandering, I have waited quietly for the salvation of the Lord, for his goodness in the dark, his saving hand upon my heart.

Surely I can be confident that he will be faithful to his Word; his promises stay to a thousand generations (Deuteronomy 7:9). My God has been good to me, in the places where it has not felt good. But his presence was ever before me (Matthew 28:20), leading me, walking with me, assuring me even when I couldn't see.

The goodness of the Lord in the land of the living is a gift given a hundred times over, and the awe with which it is received never diminishes.

Close your eyes. Breathe in the Lord. Can you sense his goodness?

He is Immanuel, God with us in the miracle moments that make us hold to him even more. We can pull up our strength to wait and trust and see the God who sees us through, look for his fingerprints, sense his breath on our necks, evidence of him in the swirl of love around us in his natural world and in the ones we call beloved. He sees us through, through the fire and the rising waters, through the fear and fog. The Lord is gracious, even when it seems upside down. But his kingdom is here, already at work (Luke 17:20-21)—at work in us.

Where can we go where he is not? Already, he is in the heights and depths (Psalm 139:7-8), and when darkness stretches over us, we take heart in his light, for even the darkness is not dark to him (Psalm 139:12).

The Lord is good to those who place their trust in him, and he never leaves the righteous forsaken (Psalm 37:25). His heart is pure, his love is life, and his plans are purposeful and heaven led. When the waters rise or the heat heightens, remain confident that he does appear, bends close to build us up in our weakness and expand our faith, our love for him.

To wait on the Lord is to exhibit faith that's formed deep within our frame, from the tenderness of his mercies to a tired but expectant heart.

I remain confident of this: I will see the goodness of the Lord *in the land of the living.*
Wait for the Lord*; be strong and take heart and wait for the* Lord.

PSALM 27:13-14

A light streams into this feeble heart, sure and clean. A light streams in to say we are seen, we are held, that this has always been the way. And the way out of the valley is through the good guidance of our Shepherd, who gives us what we need and leads us by his love.

Yes, it is quite okay to be happy. To experience joy, sustaining grace, the goodness of our God who beautifully moves in the land of the living. To rejoice in the light of the Lord and let him lead us further into the life in full he offers (John 10:10).

Yes, the Lord has been good, has been my salvation, my strength. This is his promise for now, forever.

REFLECT

Where have you seen the goodness of the Lord?

What would it look like to live even deeper in his goodness?
How does celebrating this goodness encourage your faith?

LINGER

Ezra 3:11; Psalm 27:1; Psalm 139:1-6

RESPOND

Oh Lord, you have been so faithful. Through all the ups and downs, twists and turns, you have been with me in the valley. Thank you for sheltering me and showing me the way deeper into your heart. I'm grateful that I can remain confident of your goodness in the land of the living. You are my greatest treasure, the one who sustains me. In Jesus' name, amen.

PRAISE

"Goodness of God" by Jenn Johnson

47

THE ONE WHO SATISFIES

Relaxing into Jesus' Rest

SATISFIED. **MATTHEW 15:37**

God nourishes us like nothing else can. Our human longing for an eternal solution leads us to gulp down cheap offerings that do nothing to nourish. True longings go far deeper than any material hunger, and though we try our best to fill ourselves with what feels good in the moment, it later leaves us looking for more.

Remember God and how all he gives is greater than anything we could ever come up with on our own. He is the one who satisfies the sting of hunger pains deep within our bellies, who smooths the sharpness of our souls.

When all the air of the day has been exhaled, what's left is the rumble of our spiritual and emotional hunger, where we pull up a seat at the table of God's love and abundance, relaxing our tight grip on our worries and receive his beckoning to his care. Here, he takes us as we are, with nothing left, childlike in our need for his sustenance and soothing love.

Jesus always has compassion in abundance for both our spiritual and practical needs. When he and his throngs of followers found themselves on a mountainside for ministry, much was happening throughout the day that led to deep hunger. Hunger for miracles, healing, and teaching that touched the needs of hearts. But the greatest needs still lingered.

> Jesus called his disciples to him and said, "I have compassion for these people; they have already been with me three days and have nothing to eat. I do not want to send them away hungry, or they may collapse on the way."
>
> His disciples answered, "Where could we get enough bread in this remote place to feed such a crowd?"
>
> "How many loaves do you have?" Jesus asked.
>
> "Seven," they replied, "and a few small fish."
>
> He told the crowd to sit down on the ground. Then he took the seven loaves and the fish, and when he had given thanks, he broke them and gave them to the disciples, and they in turn to the people. They all ate and were satisfied. Afterward the disciples picked up seven basketfuls of broken pieces that were left over. The number of those who ate was four thousand men, besides women and children (Matthew 15:32-38).

The number of men, women, and children who ate their fill of the loaves and fish was more than 4,000. Making provision for so many is a grand-scale miracle, but so much of Jesus' ministry happened one-on-one with a person who came to him and expressed a need. Jesus saw them and attended to what hurt them while also restoring their soul. God cares about the wellbeing of the many, but he's also invested in satisfying each of our individual needs. This means you and your yearning to be seen and understood. This means me and my insatiable desire for love and belonging.

After Jesus gave thanks for what was given, the disciples distributed a meal that sustained and satisfied the large crowd. While he met them in their spiritual need, he also met them in their physical need, because that was also important. And he meets us in all our needs because he knows what we hunger for can only be found in him.

When we hold our hands and hearts out to God, he will fill them with what he wants to give. When we recognize the lover of our souls gives bountiful provision, we can receive more easily the peace, presence, hope, and healing when we are swept in the song of his delight and let his voice wash over us.

Jesus did great work with hungry people. Think of what he can do when you come to him with a beautiful expectation of him satisfying your deepest needs.

They all ate and were satisfied.

MATTHEW 15:37

May this be our call of faith, to believe in the beautiful provision of the Lord. To take satisfaction in the way he loves us, settles us, bathes us in his love. His fulfillment is gentle, soft, soothing , relaxing. It is tender, taking great care. There is no rush, there is only relationship. To come to Jesus, the one who knows our need, the hunger pangs of our hearts and has the power and ability to satisfy.

We are safe when we bring ourselves to him. Jesus never leaves us lacking.

REFLECT

What are the longings of your heart? How can you take those longings to the Lord?

Trust that Jesus is at work in you to satisfy in ways that only he can. Is there anything you are holding back that you haven't yet entrusted to him?

LINGER

Psalm 37:3-4; Matthew 5:6; Philippians 4:19

RESPOND

Lord, you are the only one who satisfies. I've been looking for fulfillment in places that still leave me hungry. I long for deeper satisfaction through what you have to give. Help me take my needs to you and believe that you are at work to bring me what I truly need. Only you can meet the longing of my heart. In Jesus' name, amen.

PRAISE

"Hunger (Live)" by CeCe Winans

48

GROWN SO LOVELY

Continuing to Blossom in Christ

REMAIN IN ME. **JOHN 15:4**

In those first signs of life after winter's long sleep, I see the beauty of life blooming: unfurling petals, buds slowly opening, and the stretching of vines, lifelines of beauty and fruit bearing. My neighbor has a beautiful garden; she tends to the plants and flowers, knows all their names and how to best care for them. She lovingly spends time tending the soil, preparing the environment for the fullness of her garden again. And then she lets the sun, the soil, and the passing of time do their work. She's intentional, but she knows when to yield control to nature. She can pour in effort, but not everything is up to her.

As spring awakens within us, we can step closer to God. Closer, so we can feel his breath on our skin, feel the rhythm of his heartbeat, receive the care and nourishment he lavishes upon our growing places. We have the ability to cultivate lasting fruit in our lives, if we choose to plant our hearts in the soil of Scripture and allow God to water, tend, and prune. God can grow fruit that makes an eternal impact in us (Galatians 5:22-23) as we allow him all access to our minds, bodies, hearts, and souls.

In order for this fruit to form, we must be attached to the source from which all things grow:

I am the true vine, and my Father is the gardener. He cuts off every branch in me that bears no fruit, while every branch that does bear fruit he prunes so that it will be even more fruitful. You are already clean because of the word I have spoken to you. Remain in me, as I also remain in you. No branch can bear fruit by itself; it must remain in the vine. Neither can you bear fruit unless you remain in me.

I am the vine; you are the branches. If you remain in me and I in you, you will bear much fruit; apart from me you can do nothing. If you do not remain in me, you are like a branch that is thrown away and withers; such branches are picked up, thrown into the fire and burned. If you remain in me and my words remain in you, ask whatever you wish, and it will be done for you. This is to my Father's glory, that you bear much fruit, showing yourselves to be my disciples.

As the Father has loved me, so have I loved you. Now remain in my love (John 15:1-9).

How lovely we grow when tended to by the Gardener of our souls. When we stay in step with him, branch to vine, heart to heart. Apart from him we can do nothing, and in him we have everything.

Intimacy goes both ways; there is always room for us to draw nearer, give him more of ourselves, and let him see our vulnerabilities. He is always after our hearts; he is patient, kind, selfless, and always thinking of our best. In return, may we be as vulnerable and open, as bold in our love. May we be unafraid to lay our feelings on the line and let him in to the deeper parts of our hearts.

His heart is true; he can be trusted. He doesn't change; he is always for us, always longing for more of us. So, here we are, willing and wanting to share all we are with him. To give our life and our soul, to look to him for where we should go, and to learn more about the light of his love. He encourages us to press in, deeper still. It's our decision to draw near or step away, our choice to come or go; his heart is already wide open and waiting (James 4:8).

Wouldn't it be beautiful to have even *more* knowledge of who God is, how he views the world and what our place in it is? But not just through knowing, but through being planted deep within?

Grow in the grace and knowledge of our
Lord and Savior Jesus Christ.
To him be glory both now and forever! Amen.

2 PETER 3:18

We can remain in his love and let him be our beloved; we can choose to fall into his arms and nestle in safe and steady, to abide in his love, the steadfast, unending, and unchanging gift of himself, given with grace.

There is no better place to be than coiled securely in his love. May our hearts be his as we remain under his wise and fruitful care, abiding in the shadow of his wing (Psalm 91:1, 4), taking shelter, receiving solace from the one who knows our wiring well. The more we abide in him, the more he remains in us too, until we are tangled as one, drinking from the stream of the life he gives us, waiting for the right timing of ripeness and readiness to flourish in the world.

We have grown so lovely in the hands of our God. May we nestle in closer still, remaining secure in the garden of his heart.

REFLECT

What fruit of the Spirit (love, joy, peace, forbearance, kindness, goodness, faithfulness, gentleness, self-control) (Galatians 5:22-23) would you like more of in your life? Ask God to cultivate these fruits!

How can you abide even closer in the life and love of Jesus?

LINGER

2 Thessalonians 2:16-17; 1 John 2:28; 1 John 3:24

RESPOND

Lord, thank you that I can abide in you, and that is the best place for me to be. Apart from you I can do nothing, even though I try to take matters into my own hands. Help me stay connected to you and cultivate the fruit of the Spirit in my life. I love you, Lord, and I thank you that you see me and love me. In Jesus' name, amen.

PRAISE

"Abide" by Christy Nockels

49

HIS GOODNESS HAS REMAINED

Reflecting on the Wonder of God

HE REMAINS FAITHFUL. **PSALM 146:6**

It's a reminder when I walk out of valleys and into seasons of sun: the Lord has always gone before me. Through nights of tears and trudging through unyielding days, God has been my compass when I have lost my way. I look back on my years of pain and see his light shining through, leading me like a bright star in the evening sky. When I've had reasons to rejoice, his face has been what I've seen in my gratitude. My God's goodness has followed me all of my days (Psalm 23:6).

He has been there for you too. Look back and remember. Where have you seen the steady presence of the Lord? How has he stuck by you in your times of trouble, and delighted with you in times of joy? We who take shelter in his love are blessed.

Blessed are those whose help is in the God of Jacob, whose hope is in the Lord their God.
He is the Maker of heaven and earth, the sea, and everything in them—he remains faithful forever.

PSALM 146:5-6

His faithfulness is a guiding light, clear and illuminating, reminding us that we are never alone, no matter how dark the night may be or how far off course we've strayed. It projects a glowing beacon that can be seen far from the shore, where we spy from our wave-tossed boats a steadfast light to lead us home, where we'll be enveloped by the warm refuge of his embrace (Psalm 91:4).

His goodness is a sturdy lifeline that has saved us more times than we know. He's held us up when we've been sinking, flailing in the water, tossed along by the weight of waves. His goodness has remained, pulling us back to his side, keeping us steady. What a joy when we are lifted from the tempest and set safely in his arms! Even in our deepest despair, in the unexpected shattering of life and dreams, his everlasting love keeps us steady (Lamentations 3:22-23).

He is our Helper. He is mighty to save, gentle with our hearts, true to his promises. He guides us when our map rips and the coordinates smudge, when we are standing in the unknown and unable to see where to go. He sets us out on our journey, where he continues to lead us well and walk beside us, directing us to find the ways that are best and quieting chaos into calm when the winds become overwhelming.

He is our hope. In him, we no longer need to fear the end, for everything in this life is only the beginning. He reminds us that he will hold onto our deepest hopes and most secret dreams; he asks us to remember he has our best in mind. He has taught us to trust, to hand over our hearts to be kept in his capable hands. He assures our skittish souls that he is here, seeing us, standing with us. He gives us a hope that is eternally secure, and also hope that meets us right here in the middle of this life.

Yes, my soul, find rest in God; my hope comes from him.
Truly he is my rock and my salvation; he is my fortress,
I will not be shaken.

PSALM 62:5-6

His presence brings peace. We notice him in the sliver of light coming through our curtains when the day is stirring us from sleep; we are reminded of him in the drying flowers on our table still fighting for beauty, the smooth dance of flame from a morning candle. Our God has never forsaken us and has only drawn closer, longed for more of our love. While we have strayed at times, forgetting our worth and trying to find it in cracked and crooked places, he has always stayed and spoken the truth of our identity into us. Waiting, watching, loving us with everything he is, ready to receive us back into his embrace when we realize whose we really are.

He is the one who sees, the one who stays, the one who fights for what is his. Blessed are we to find our help in him, to find that we can hope with brightest trust, grounded by a foundation that will not be shaken. We turn to his beauty, his wisdom, his wonder. Deeper into his heart do we run. He remains faithful; we remain his.

REFLECT

How has God been faithful to you over the years? Where have you most recently noticed his faithfulness in your life?

How has God's goodness shaped your faith? What are some examples of his goodness that you've witnessed or experienced?

LINGER

Psalm 36:5; Psalm 145:9; Colossians 3:16

RESPOND

God, over all this time, you still love me just as much as you did from the beginning. Thank you for your faithfulness, your lovingkindness, your goodness, and your presence. Thank you that you never leave me, and that you give me great hope for what's to come. Give my heart more of you, please. I want to be closer; I want more of a relationship with you. You are my God, and I praise and love you. In Jesus' name, amen.

PRAISE

"I Know You Are Good" by The Church Will Sing

50

GREAT IS HIS FAITHFULNESS

Remembering the Journey

HIS COMPASSIONS NEVER FAIL. **LAMENTATIONS 3:22-23**

September 2024

Early morning sunlight slants in through the oval window 33,000 feet above the ground. The sun appears closer as the plane streams through the sky on its course southwest from Milwaukee to Kansas City.

Being up here gives me time to think, to remember. There were days when I didn't think I'd travel again, either from life situations that kept me grounded, physical sickness where I fought to remain alive, or my own mental instability that caused tears to stream down my face when I considered stepping on a plane and leaving Eric to place myself alone at the mercy of my fears.

The winds of life have let me feel the sting of suffering, yet these winds have also carried me straight to the solid and safe person of Jesus.

I look back on the previous years' storms and how they tried to take me under. Yet here I am, sipping coffee and marveling at the wonder that is air transportation, the wonder that God has brought me this far, back to what I love.

He lifted me out of the slimy pit, out of the mud and mire;
he set my feet on a rock and gave me a firm place to stand.

PSALM 40:2

Here we all are, holding on because we've held to him. His faithfulness endures, his protective arms spread over us, establishing a deeper perspective of the valley.

This is our God who walks with us through the valley, who admits we will go through fire and flood, but he gives us his Word to walk with us through them. Where our feet slip, he catches us and sets us on solid ground. When we falter, his Spirit strengthens our inner being to endure. When we doubt, he is still gracious to come through again and again. Our God is a safe space, a refuge that warms our weary hearts, and a guiding light that steers our battered boats to the safety of shore.

Can you see him at work in your life? When you were in the shadows that threatened your faith and wellbeing, how did his light shine through? How has he protected you in every sense? Take a step back and remember.

I will remember the deeds of the LORD; yes,
I will remember your miracles of long ago.
I will consider all your works and meditate
on all your mighty deeds.

PSALM 77:11-12

Let us give thanks to the Lord for he is good; his faithful love endures forever (Psalm 136).

As we begin the descent through the clouds, I watch the ribbons of river below weave through the patchwork landscape. Things look so different from up here. Perspective shifts when I can see the world in a new way.

When we give a little distance from our daily struggles and situations, God's lens allows us to see beyond the immediate and catch a glimpse of what he is doing for the long haul. His hand weaving a patchwork tapestry out of our trials, his heart lovingly shaping ours in a beautiful refinement that cascades his love and grace into the world. Our hurts are really healing us, weaving hope in our souls and holding a harder-earned faith in he who first hovered over the waters (Genesis 1:2) and then our hearts.

Because of the Lord's great love we are not consumed,
for his compassions never fail. They are new every
morning; great is your faithfulness.
LAMENTATIONS 3:22-23

Because of his great love we are not consumed but covered in his compassion. Great is his love, his purpose, his beauty, and his grace. Great is his faithfulness. Now and forever.

REFLECT

Think of your storms, your valleys. What threatened to take you under? Now, look to the Lord. Where did you see him in your story? How has he sustained you?

Remember how God has led you through this journey when you're on your next journey with him. How might what you've recently learned encourage you later? How might sharing your story be an encouragement to others?

LINGER

Deuteronomy 7:9; Isaiah 25:1; 2 Timothy 2:13

RESPOND

Lord, what a journey. What a life. All along, you were there. With me in the heartache, in the hopeless days, in the never-ending nights. Because of your great love I am not consumed; I am yours. Your compassions never fail; great is your faithfulness to me. I praise you because you are worthy of it all, powerful and strong, kind, and gentle. Great is your faithfulness! In Jesus' name, amen.

PRAISE

"Great Is Thy Faithfulness" by Worship Circle and Christy Nockels

CLOSING

A Quiet in the Setting Sun

Look at us—we are here, together, with him. The waters may have rushed over us, but they did not overtake us. The fires raged, but neither skin nor soul were singed.

We've made it through the valley of hard things, blinking our eyes in wonder at the stretch of sun lighting our path as we find our footing up the peak.

When you pass through the waters, I will be with you;
and when you pass through the rivers, they will not
sweep over you. When you walk through the fire, you
will not be burned; the flames will not set you ablaze.

ISAIAH 43:2

We've set our hearts on pilgrimage and God has guided us through (Psalm 84:5).

We've put our hope in God, and he does not disappoint us (Romans 5:5).

He is the Good Shepherd who promises and commits to seeing us through (John 10:11).

Isn't it amazing how he stays true to his Word? Isn't it incredible how he enables us to not only endure, but thrive?

We've come a long way. Through the night watches (Psalm 63:6), we've learned to recognize the voice of the Shepherd, tuned our ears to hear the beat of his heart and know the comforting pressure of his hand. Like Jacob, we can say, "Surely the LORD is in this place" (Genesis 28:16).

The Lord has indeed been in these places of burden with us, and while it may not have felt good, let's acknowledge the good within because he was there. There is goodness when we are with God, experiencing him in new ways, deeper truths developed in our hearts that will carry us into the days ahead.

There will be days that threaten our well-won faith, our peace, and our joy. But remembering how God has come through before will sustain us in believing that he will come through again.

His goodness is guaranteed. His presence is here, one heartbreaking yet holy moment at a time.

Praise be to the Lord, to God our Savior,
who daily bears our burdens.

PSALM 68:19

ACKNOWLEDGMENTS

How can I begin to talk about the people who mean so much to this writer's heart? I feel like this page is harder to write than the book itself!

To my editor, Emma Saisslin, who believed in this project and in me. I will aways remember getting an email from you asking if I'd consider turning my book concept into a devotional—God was breathing life into something I had only dared to hope for and gave you eyes to see it. *Thank you.*

To the Harvest House team, you are a joy to work with. Thank you for believing in this project and giving it life with all your vision and talents. It's a gift to do this together.

My Morning Glory women, Janet and Molly, you are sisters in Christ and treasured friends. Thank you for always believing in my words and cheering me on, and for your countless prayers.

My Misfits—Kara, Lauren, and Heidi—we have been through the mountains and valleys together, looking to God and giving one another grace.

Sarah B., so glad to be journeying this life with you. Thank you for your faith, joy, wisdom, and friendship.

To the Proverbs 31 team, I am immensely grateful for you taking a chance on me, first with Compel, then as part of the Encouragement for Today devotions team. It's because of your graciousness in giving writers opportunities to grow in their craft that this book is in people's hands.

All my writing friends and the women of Redbud Writers Guild—I am better because of you.

My family—when you see one Rennicke, you see them all. Mom, Dad, Randy and Steph, Jordan and Mandy, Bekah and Ian, Charlie, Clayton, Micah, Rhodes, Jonas, and baby girl, when I think about you, words feel shallow. I cannot properly put into thought all that your love, encouragement, and support have meant. Thank you for putting up with a broody Enneagram 4 in her adolescence, and for all the birthdays I ruined. I hope putting you in the acknowledgments makes up for that!

Rick and Patti Freymuth, thank you for welcoming me into the family and allowing me to love your son. You raised a gentleman, and it's an honor to carry your name.

Eric—you opened the drawer to my dreams and wouldn't let me close it. What a privilege it is to go through life with you. I love you more than I could ever say. You are my favorite.

And to my Lord—this has been *our* journey from the beginning. You have been so faithful. All glory to you.

ABOUT THE AUTHOR

Sarah Freymuth is the content and storytelling manager for Fellowship of Christian Athletes, and she writes for numerous platforms, including Proverbs 31 Ministries, YouVersion, (in)Courage, and She Reads Truth. Sarah loves unearthing God's goodness in places that don't feel good, with a heart especially for faith and mental health. She enjoys a simple Wisconsin life by Lake Michigan with her husband, Eric, and Beaglier pup, Alfie Hitchcock.